ADVANCE PRAISE

"Nils Elmark has a rare talent for revealing the next step in fintech development before anyone else does. He has a unique overview of fintech and has guided our readers for years on an exciting journey through a financial universe where change happens faster than ever before."
Svein Åge Eriksen, Editor in Chief, *Finansfokus*

"Nils Elmark has, over many years, written a series of excellent articles and thought-provoking columns about fintech in our magazine. He has explored London's evolving fintech jungle and introduced us to successful challenger banks and exciting fintech start-ups. He has given our readers new insight in the latest financial technology and shown incumbent banks the way forwards. *The New Local Economy* similarly provides lively and sharp insight into future finance."
Carsten Jørgensen, Editor in Chief, *The Finans Magazine*

"Most people who are Nils' age have no clue about technology or the way finance works today, let alone the way it will work in the future. They rarely think outside of the box within which they operate. The opposite is true of Nils. He's a traveller who easily switches between worlds, be it between countries, like Denmark or Great Britain, or mindsets, like classic banking, fintech or crypto development. Wherever he goes he keeps his eyes open, full of hunger and curiosity for what is to come. It's this 360° curiosity which makes him such an inspiring person who manages to convey his thinking to people, no matter their level of expertise."
Stefanie Milcke, Vice President of Marketing and Communications, ndgit

"Nils is the most creative and innovative person I have ever met! He inspires you to do new and different things. I would recommend Nils to anyone who feels they are lacking in innovative spirit. Nils has the power to move companies as well as municipalities – as long as you have the courage to follow him."
Elisabeth Grüner, Politician and Social Democrat

"Nils' passion, enthusiasm and accuracy in foreseeing what is yet to come is astounding. His creativity, interest and real love for humanity within communities is both moving and inspiring. Nils' commitment to viewing the truth from every angle makes this man unique and brave. Once met, never forgotten – I have only love for this very special man."
Sarah Parry, Founder and CEO, The What If Academy

Published by
LID Publishing Limited
The Record Hall, Studio 204,
16-16a Baldwins Gardens,
London EC1N 7RJ, UK

info@lidpublishing.com
www.lidpublishing.com

A member of:
BPR
Business Publishers Roundtable

www.businesspublishersroundtable.com

Printed in Latvia by Jelgavas Tipogrāfija
ISBN: 978-1-911498-93-3

Cover and page design: Matthew Renaudin

NILS ELMARK

THE NEW LOCAL ECONOMY

HOW THE FUTURE'S BIG BUSINESSES WILL GROW OUT OF SMALL COMMUNITIES

LID

MADRID | MEXICO CITY | LONDON
NEW YORK | BUENOS AIRES
BOGOTA | SHANGHAI | NEW DELHI

CONTENTS

INTRODUCTION

IN THE FUTURE, WE WILL NEED LOTS AND LOTS OF NEW, SMALL DREAMS

In just a decade, a handful of businesspeople with big dreams have changed the world. People like Mark Zuckerberg of Facebook, Jeff Bezos of Amazon, Tim Cook of Apple, Jack Ma of Alibaba, Larry Page of Google, Travis Kalanick of Uber and Ma Huateng of Tencent have digitized the planet, brought billions of people and businesses online and created a new way of living. This is even before we see the changes they may create with artificial intelligence (AI) once they get it up and running in a wired global brain.

This new globalized economy that tech companies are creating is not entirely in the best interests of the majority of the planet's eight billion people. You can see it by how they vote. We need much more from the future than simply what a score of businesspeople can dream up. For that, we need lots and lots of new, small dreams – billions of little dreams – that will give people hope and guide our communities in a new sustainable direction.

I am an optimist. The pendulum is about to swing back from globalization. I see emerging trends pointing towards a new modern economy that grows out of small dreams in small communities. I see examples of this trend that indicate that the next distributed economy will be just as competitive as the global centralized economy that rules now.

That is what this book is about. I will take you on a trip into a future scenario where small is a beautiful starting point. This isn't a manual, and it isn't the kind of textbook used at business schools. I want to inspire you to create your own business future. I want you to develop your own dreams and feel at ease with a highly unpredictable future. In my little narrative, I shall constantly zoom in and out, showing the big picture as I see it and pointing at little details that may have big importance.

This book builds on real-life examples and stories of trendsetting people and businesses I have met as a futurist. It is a catalogue of trends that will inspire people to reimagine their futures, make their own interpretations and bring their businesses in sync with time. And I hope that when you have seen what is possible in the future, you will be inspired to dream bigger and brighter dreams.

1

IT'S TIME TO MAKE FINTECH SMALL

Financial technology, or fintech, is the new technology that is transforming banking, finance and our entire economy. It's an innovative technology that will compete with the traditional delivery methods of financial services. In the last five years, I have followed the evolution of fintech at close range. My interest was first ignited during an event called The Kickstarter Economy, held in Shoreditch, London. It was an evening full of visions and ideas about crowdfunding, peer-to-peer lending and new types of economies. The young fintech start-ups want to correct the consequences of the financial crisis and give people and businesses new opportunities to realize their potential for the future. The keynote speakers described how fintech would soon overtake traditional banks, which would eventually disappear like cassette recorders and typewriters.

Since then, London has become one of the fintech capitals of the world, and investment in fintech has exploded from $1.8 billion in 2010 to $35 billion in 2018.

Fintech has indeed transformed banking, but not quite in the way we had expected. The big banks have not disappeared – they have grown – and the young ventures still struggle to get by.

Big international banks are clever. They have adopted new financial technology and will continue to do so. After a short period of denial – "Fintech start-ups a threat? Bah, humbug!" – the incumbents have embraced the young start-ups with their wild ideas and sophisticated financial technology. Employees, counters and branches around the world have increasingly been replaced by smartphones and mobile payments that enable banks to service their customers remotely without having to meet them face-to-face.

These new financial ideas have come from young software developers outside the financial universe. They have been attracted to the fintech ecosystems in Silicon Valley, London, Berlin, New York and Singapore. Here the young mobile geeks and technology wizards are taken under the wings of venture capitalists and big, powerful banks that trim and develop the fresh new ideas through incubators and accelerators. These new financial company factories – there are thousands around the world – operate very much like the talent competitions on TV. They scan thousands of young entrepreneurs to find the most talented nine or ten start-ups and then hone and train them in boot camps until they are ready to be let loose in front of venture funds or become integrated in the big financial institutions.

We are witnessing a battle between incredibly powerful venture capitalists and international financial institutions over the global money flow of some $2 quadrillion. Let me give an example of how the future financial infrastructure is being created.

In 2013, two young Austrian entrepreneurs, Maximilian Tayenthal and Valentin Stalf, both with broad international business backgrounds, formed N26, an online-only bank based in Berlin. They wanted to build the first European bank that exists only on the smartphone. This sounded like a good idea to Peter Thiel, one of Silicon Valley's leading venture capitalists, and Li Ka-shing, one of the richest men in China. They both invest in disruptive financial technology, and this was exactly what N26 was offering. They wanted to disrupt traditional banking.

Almost at the same time, Germany's two biggest banks, Commerzbank and Deutsche Bank, each opened their own incubators and innovation labs to develop brand-new fintech solutions and business models that would keep them competitive against the challenger banks.

This is happening everywhere in the world. With few exceptions, fintech has become the tool to make big systems even bigger or exchange one big system with another big system. But this was not the dream of those in the basement in Shoreditch five years ago. They wanted everyone to have control over their own finances. They wanted every community to be able to grow at its own pace. Neither the venture capitalists nor the big banks are to blame because we haven't achieved our initial dream, however. They are just pursuing theirs.

From the very beginning, trendsetters have tried to make fintech big. Now it is time we looked at fintech from a community perspective and started to make fintech small. New financial technologies – such as crowdfunding, peer-to-peer lending, mobile payments, AI, advanced algorithms and blockchain technology – will work just as well in a local environment as in a global one. We just have to make it a priority, which we haven't done before.

2

STUCK IN THE APPLE ECONOMY

Since Apple Inc. first launched its Macintosh computer during the third quarter of the 1984 Super Bowl game, the volume of the annual trade of goods around the globe has grown from $2 trillion to $20 trillion. Apple itself has gone from near-bankruptcy to be the most valuable company in the world. Some expect it to be the first $1 trillion company. It operates seamlessly across cultural and national borders, manufactures where it is most favourable, sells wherever possible and places its profit where the taxations are lowest.

Apple has become a role model of the modern global urbanized economy. This is how successful companies operate today. Since the financial crisis, a new generation of brands has thrived on the obsolete business structure of the 20th century. Facebook, Starbucks, Google, Amazon, Alibaba, Tencent and Apple have become representatives of a modern global economy and have been followed by a host of other huge companies operating in the same way.

It's marvellous how fast the global economy has progressed in the last decade. And we should be happy about this new *Wirtschaftswunder*, because it's in the process of pulling a large part of the global population out of poverty and into the middle class.

But something's wrong. It's as if the new urbanization sucks the energy out of its surroundings, and the global companies subsequently suck their profits out of the cities and hoard cash they don't know what to do with in their tax havens. The top five American tech companies (Apple, Microsoft, Google, Cisco and Oracle) alone have stashed away $600 billion overseas – almost like ransom money.

How can they do it? Most of the new global companies that operate in Europe are registered in the tax havens of Luxembourg or Ireland, and the majority of America's big companies are registered in states like Delaware, Nevada and Wyoming, where company taxes are almost non-existent. And their influence is growing. In 1954, the 500 largest companies created one third of the American gross domestic product (GDP); in the latest statistics, they now comprise three quarters of the GDP. This is primarily because the 100 biggest companies have grown excessively at the expense of the rest.

In the same period, the average life expectancy of American companies on Standard & Poor's top 500 list has shrunk from 61 to just 18 years. In other words, the big companies have become bigger, their lives are much shorter and they are experts in international tax evasion.

The changes of the global corporate landscape are vast and fast. Six years ago, few people had heard of Uber. Now the ride-hailing company is worth more than the auto manufacturer BMW and for a good reason: Uber and the other ride-hailing companies now generate two out of three taxi rides in New York, beating the iconic yellow cabs on their own ground. They replace professional cab drivers with amateurs and, if Uber succeeds in creating its own self-driving car, they will eventually replace the amateurs with robots.

Economists and management gurus have praised this fast, global, borderless economy, driven by new technology, with terms such as 'creative innovation' or 'creative destruction', which makes it all sound positive and, well, creative. But outside the venture capitalist ecosystems and the management schools, many communities are left extremely vulnerable. It's the real people who pay the price. The suicide rate among New York City taxi drivers is rising, and as one yellow cab driver said to *Wired* magazine: "In 2001, you could work nine hours and easily make $200 in a day. Now, you're lucky if you make $50 or $60."

This is creative disruption in full swing, and Uber is setting the rules on the new game board. It has the patent of its ride-hailing app registered in Bermuda, which enables the company to dodge taxes. Worried? These are the good times. What if we have another crisis? The last time the global economy crashed, Detroit went broke and lost half a million jobs. A decade later, the city is still trying to get back on its feet.

We are building a global economy that relies on still fewer and bigger companies that believe they are too big to fail and will live forever. They are wrong and when they fail, the consequences are dire. Look at what happened to Nokia in Finland. At its height, the company owned half the global market for mobile phones; today it has been practically eradicated. Within a few years, Nokia lost 20,000 jobs. A former employee from the city of Oulu in Northern Finland said: "We are not as bad off as they are in Greece, but we will be!" Five years after Nokia's total collapse in 2013, Oulu was still struggling with the highest unemployment rate in Finland.

In South Korea, some economists are starting to get worried about the centralized economy run by family conglomerates, the so-called *chaebols*. Samsung generates 20% of South Korea's economy and with a handful of other family-controlled *chaebols*, including Hyundai and LG, they constitute half of the country's economy. What happens if these giants crumple like Nokia?

But we are not just dependent on huge companies; we are dependent on huge systems as well.

In the summer of 2017, the Danish shipping company Maersk was hit by the computer virus Petya, which paralyzed more than 75 harbours across the world. For several days nobody knew the contents of hundreds of thousands of shipping containers. Everything was automated, and the system was down. In June 2018, the payment giant Visa had a meltdown and for a day millions of Europeans could not use their credit cards, which created chaos in shops and restaurants. One month before, 8,500 post offices in France were paralyzed for a day by a computer bug.

A sophisticated global operating system has emerged, and big companies and big technology systems control it. But even though they may be clever, we cannot put our future into the hands of Tim Cook, Mark Zuckerberg, Jack Ma, Jeff Bezos and the rest of the global business leaders who have formed the world post-2008. We have to protect a global population of eight billion people against the next potential crisis of the global economy, which, because of a decade of hyper-globalization, could be even worse than the one we experienced in 2008.

But maybe there is an even scarier scenario: *what if they succeed?* What if the global tech companies get their way with all their robots, AI, quantum computers and internet of things?

The power of new technology is going to be formidable, and the key to it all seems to be AI. As a result, most employees will become superfluous in the future; they will basically be in the way of the progress of the algorithms and the robots.

Technology has created a new playground for business, with a completely new set of rules. This started in 2007 when Apple introduced the iPhone. A lot of people and businesses thought it was the financial crisis that changed the world. It wasn't. It was just an unfortunate event that made room for the breakthrough of new ideas and business models growing on the platform of the smartphone. With the smartphone, android and iOS, everything changed: the way we communicate with family and friends, the way we get elected into the White House, the way we shop, pay for stuff, seek information, are entertained and find our way about on the planet.

The smartphone and the technologies attached to it define the new global business playground. The majority of businesses are stuck on the old playground; they are out of sync with modern times and struggle to cross the gap that has grown into a chasm. If they get across, they often play by the old rules and will eventually shrink until they disappear. As the super venture capitalist Peter Thiel explains in his book *Zero to One* (co-written with Blake Masters), Twitter's initial public offering (IPO) in 2013 created a market cap of $24 billion, which was 12 times as much as the value of The New York Times Company. The two companies were both in the news business, they had a similar number of employees and The New York Times Company even had a profit of $133 million, whereas Twitter had a deficit.

Why was Twitter much more valuable? Because investors expected a growing cash flow from Twitter for the next ten years, whereas they questioned whether The New York Times Company would still exist in a decade.

The figures have changed for Twitter and The New York Times Company since Peter Thiel wrote his book. Now Twitter is only five times as valuable, but the pattern is the same when comparing old companies with the new 21st-century players.

Barclays employs 130,000 people and has a market value of $48 billion; PayPal employs 13,000 people and has a market value of $96 billion. The two companies do more or less the same thing: move other people's money around. But Barclays needs ten times as many people and is only worth half the value of PayPal on the stock exchange. The new generation of global companies are ten to 20 times more efficient than the old ones. So, if we don't invent new jobs, the number of jobs in our communities will dwindle – or may even be decimated.

People are getting scared. They can see and feel the consequences of the surging urbanized and globalized tech-driven economy that takes away jobs and capital – money that is earned in a community in which it is never going to be reinvested. The reaction has been to vote for leaders whose names we didn't know just a few years ago, but who promise to turn back time. For businesses, the reaction has been head-over-heel investments in new technology without vision – and cutting people, of course. We have gone into protection mode; we have been listening to the narratives of venture capitalists and tech companies in Silicon Valley, London Tech City and Beijing. We measure success by counting 'unicorns', which are start-ups worth more than a billion dollars. In 2018, there were 236 venture-backed unicorns, of which 27 were fintech companies, according to the research company CB Insights. We count and idolize these investment superstars, but almost every time a unicorn is created, power becomes centralized by a handful of venture capitalists waiting for their next exit.

And our communities are paying the price. This is why we need to create a new narrative that brings the local communities across the gap and onto the new modern tech platform of the 21st century. We need to create a new, robust type of economy that will allow everyone to grow – a new 'business operating system' that will bring hope to millions of people and support coming generations to dream brave dreams and look forward to the future without fear.

3

BIG BANKS – BURDENED BY THEIR OWN WEIGHT

In 2008, governments all over the world had to intervene to save the global banking system from total collapse. The price tag on the financial crisis is $22 trillion in America alone, and in the UK taxpayers had to chip in £1 trillion to save the stranded banks. The financial infrastructure of the West was about to disintegrate and, despite strict legislation and increased governmental regulations, the situation hasn't really improved. Europe's big banks are still in a horrible state and the market value decimated, with the news agency Bloomberg calling them "Europe's Zombie Banks".

In 1984, the US had around 14,000 banks. Now it has 6,000 banks, and the market share of local banks has fallen from 38% to 14%. The 100 largest American banks now control 80% of the market and the four largest banks are 150% bigger than the next 50 banks combined. In the UK it's even worse, with the four biggest banks controlling 85% of the market.

This trend towards consolidating financial infrastructure is ubiquitous. Small banks disappear and big banks become bigger and the distance to customers grows. A Citigroup report expects the consolidation to continue for a decade. More than one million bank employees have already been sacked since 2008, and a further two million financial jobs are expected to disappear.

The urbanized global economy is reflected perfectly in the financial sector. As French economist Thomas Piketty wrote in his book, *Capital in the 21st Century*: "There is an inherent systemic fault in our capitalism, which means that the rich get richer and the wealth in the world is distributed unevenly. Capitalism and banking create tension on all levels."

At some point, this tension in society will inevitably become so strong that the trend of 30 years of globalization and urbanization will be broken. Every time a trend grows stronger, a new opposite trend emerges and pulls the development in a new direction. We see the signs of this growing tension everywhere in the world right now. The Americans elected Trump for president out of sheer desperation, and Trump started conflicts with US trade partners out of desperation. The British voted for an exit from the European Union out of desperation.

At the moment, Europe is experiencing the biggest migrant crisis ever, and millions of people from the Middle East and Africa are desperately trying to get into Europe. Here, as in the US, the immediate reactions have been demands for higher walls and stronger leaders. But that won't be a sustainable solution for the 21st century, where the ruling trend is borderless connectivity.

According to economist Hernando de Soto, the wave of migrants isn't created by religion or lack of freedom. It is caused by an obsolete and insufficient local and regional financial infrastructure. If capital had found its way to the poor areas of the Middle East and investments had been made in schools, businesses and housing, people would not have emigrated. But the money went by and ended up in skyscrapers and football teams in London, Dubai and other cities in the global economy.

Piketty claims that there is too much capitalism, de Soto claims there is too little, and if we could provide capital to everyone much tension would go away. But they both report about the tension that globalization is creating. As do voters across the Western world.

It's always fascinating to follow a mega-trend but, as a futurist, it is much more fascinating to look for the opposing trend that will challenge the present powerful globalized economy. You won't find it on Wall Street or in the City of London. But it is there, and we have to go to local communities to detect a new emerging trend with the potential to overtake the economy of the trillion-dollar companies.

THE GROWING NEED FOR LOCAL BANKS

In 2013, the Scottish government published a report titled "Sustainable, Responsible Banking", which documented that 70% of the country's small businesses were serviced by just two banks. The problem is that the UK in general, and Scotland in particular, is dependent on a handful of listed banks whose owners demand the highest possible profit, which is badly out of sync with servicing small businesses in little towns.

From 2013 to 2014, The Royal Bank of Scotland closed 400 branches, 165 of which were "the last bank in town". During the last decade, 25% of all bank branches in the UK have closed and 1,500 communities are now unbanked.

A 2016 Scottish report, "Banking for the Common Good", underlines that the big banks are structurally unsuited to react to local needs because the decision-making has been moved from local experts to main offices, where saying "yes" to a loan is based on algorithms. This affects poor and vulnerable people and businesses without a credit history.

Over a period of 18 months, The Royal Bank of Scotland reduced its loans to small- and medium-sized enterprises (SMEs) by £2 billion. But does this really matter? Yes, says the report: SMEs in Scotland represent more than half of all jobs, and dwindling investments will have a huge impact on local communities.

Seen from a European perspective, the situation may be even more precarious. Before the financial crisis, banks in Europe gave, on average, €75 billion in loans to SMEs. In 2008, these loans actually peaked at €94 billion. Now, ten years later, the entire value of loans from European financial institutions to SMEs has fallen to €54 billion. With regard to SMEs, the European banking industry has lost one third of its effectiveness. This development may have strengthened the banks and made them more robust and able to survive the next financial crisis, but in the process of protecting the incumbent banking industry, it is about to lose its reason for being. Why do we need banks in the 21st century if those banks cannot or will not lend money to businesses? SMEs need money; they are the backbone of Europe, constitute 99% of the EU's businesses and account for 67% of all jobs.

In other words, the oxygen supply to Europe's businesses has been reduced by €21 billion a year, which equals €200 billion in total since the financial crisis. This helps to explain the missing job creation in Europe and the staggering GDP.

The situation is similar in the US. Just 25 years ago, community banks provided 75% of all consumer loans. Since then, local banks have come under pressure from the big banks and now only 9% of all consumer loans come from local banks. Since the financial crisis, almost 2,000 American banks have vanished, and the number of small community banks has dwindled by almost 40%. In 2017 American branch closures set a historic record of 1,700.

For ten years, legislators and financial decision makers all over the world have asked the question: How can we protect our banking industry and ensure that the too-big-to-fail-banks survive the next financial crisis?

That is the wrong question! The question should be: How can banking catch up on ten years of insufficient business lending, maintain a new and higher level for the future, and at the same time remove the risk of a new financial meltdown?

If financial institutions do not reinterpret themselves and regain their professional purpose in society, communities, people and businesses will search for alternative solutions.

Of the banking activities in the UK, 97% are controlled by listed national and international banks and only 3% by local community banks. According to the report "Banking for the Common Good" by the New Economics Foundation, this is the key problem with the UK's banking system. It has an overwhelming financial centralization, which leads to financial exclusion and focuses on short-term profit at the expense of local customers.

A new report from Denmark, "A Monetary System For Everybody", written by an organization called Good Money, claims that we have learned nothing from the latest financial crisis. In particular, the report revolts over the way money is created in modern society. "Most people believe that it is the central banks that make new money, but that is wrong," Professor Ole Bjerg at Copenhagen Business School says. "The central bank prints the cash we use in daily life, but that is only 5% of the total amount of money in society. The rest is digital account money that only exists as bank deposits.

"Banks create new money the moment you go into a bank and ask for a £200,000 loan. Then the bank adds that amount to your account and writes into their own account that now you owe them £200,000. Click! In that very moment, £200,000 is fuelled into the economy, and you can invest it in a new house, where prices will continue to rise as long as banks are allowed to create their own money."

For this reason, some economists have referred to bank deposits as 'fountain-pen money', created at the stroke of bankers' pens when they approve loans. Professor Bjerg believes that the central banks of the world should reclaim their role as the only rightful creators of new money, as they were a couple of centuries ago when paper money was introduced. And all citizens should have their current accounts with the central banks. Then the commercial banks would become pure financial service providers that couldn't provide more loans than the funds received in deposits.

It all sounds very radical and utopian – and I can't understand all the implications – but, as with the current financial system, where banks creating new money increases the risk of housing bubbles, his ideas should be given some attention. We are in the beginning of a new century and a new digital age. It would be wrong to simply extend old industrial thinking into the future. As Professor Bjerg said in an interview in the Danish newspaper *Politiken*: "In the past ten years, I have made almost as much money owning a house as going to work each morning. This is not a healthy society, and it has to stop!"

Another problem is the fees and interest that borrowers pay the banks. When big international banks create new money, fees and interest from local lenders are flowing away from their communities. In contrast, if a loan is taken out from a local bank, interest and fees stay in the area where the money is reinvested.

If you compare the UK banking structure to the one in Germany, you get a completely different picture. In Germany, cooperative banks, plus local and regional banks owned by the public, constitute 66% of the German financial market, and only 33% of the banks are listed and privately owned.

This distributed banking system may be one of the reasons the German economy was the first to bounce back after 2008, and the UK was the last of the G8 countries to do so. Germany has 409 local *Sparkassen* (savings banks) and 11 regional *Landesbanken* (state-owned banks) that ensure a regional balanced development for both local communities and the various federal states. The *Sparkassen* are only allowed to do business within their local community; for services that require more banking power and advanced skills, they collaborate with the much bigger *Landesbank*. This structure has created stable development of German businesses since the financial crisis, not least for SMEs.

The report "Banking For the Common Good" suggests a new UK banking structure in line with that of Germany and Switzerland. In the UK, the think tank Demos made similar suggestions in 2015, as have numerous reports over the last decade.

This decentralized financial infrastructure is found in all the Scandinavian countries. A country like Denmark, with a population of 5.5 million – half the size of London's – has 80 independent banks and *Sparkassen*. Yet even here the distributed banking model is under pressure from the bigger banks and their economies of scale. Since the financial crisis, small local banks have lost 40% market share and the ten biggest banks have gone from being five times to ten times as big as the rest of the banks combined.

In all of these examples, apart from not being where they are needed, the centralized banks do the same as the borderless companies. They attract revenues to the cities where they are registered and reinvest the money earned where the future profits seem most favourable – and that is not necessarily in small local communities or small businesses.

The challenge is that everyone basically loves local banks, which in their present form obviously cannot compete with the big banks, simply due to economies of scale. Therefore, as we see around the world, local community banks are being outperformed by the bigger and incumbent financial institutions.

Anders Bouvin, the former head of Handelsbanken (a Swedish bank) in the UK, said in an interview on

BBC Radio 4 that when you are a big bank, you tend to look at local branches as a distribution network, whereas a local branch of Handelsbanken *is* the bank. The bank has a 'church spire' philosophy, which means that the head of a local branch of Handelsbanken is solely responsible for all business and all decisions made in his local area – as far as the eye can see from the top of the church spire. This is very much like the German *Sparkassen* model, and it is claimed to be one of the reasons for the overwhelming success that the Swedish bank has had in the UK. It is close to its market and can react to customer needs.

Communities need banking, but community banks need a new business model too. As The Royal Bank of Scotland explained when it closed 167 branches in 2018: "Forty per cent fewer customers come into our branches while they manage banking from their computer or smartphone!" Handelsbanken may have one way of doing it, but there are so many other opportunities that need to be identified and tested in the coming years. The British Metro Bank has an interesting business model that seems to be working too.

Metro Bank was founded in 2010. According to founder Vernon Hill, it was the first new high street bank chartered in England "since Queen Victoria moved into the new Buckingham Palace in 1837". It's an amazing and highly extraordinary bank doing ordinary banking.

If the fast-food chain McDonald's were to open a bank, it would probably look a bit like Metro Bank. American banker Vernon Hill allegedly first intended to open his new bank in Australia, but when he had difficulties getting his dog into the country, he decided to go for Britain instead, and it has become an overwhelming success. In a period where every other bank in the country has closed branches, Metro Bank has opened branches, or rather 'stores', which is Metro-speak for branches. Customers are called 'fans'. Since its launch in 2010, Metro has opened 56 new stores and gained more than a million new fans, and the bank is profitable. Its first store was in Holborn in London, and it has since spiralled its network to cover most of southeast England. New branches are always opened not too far away from old ones, so staff from existing stores can move into the new store and ensure that the Metro-culture is transferred. And that is a culture of extremely high personal customer focus.

New employees are hired for attitude and trained for skills. If applicants have a strong personal service gene, it doesn't matter if they know nothing about banking – the bank will teach them the skills they lack. "Getting fans, not customers" is not just a slogan in the board-room, it permeates the entire organization. Regardless of which store you enter, you get the feeling of being welcome. Dogs and bicycles are often brought inside the bank, there are magic machines counting people's coins, new credit cards are 3D-printed on site, and the stores are open when fans need them, i.e. between 8am to 8pm all year round except at Christmas. Business fans can use the bank for meetings with clients, and it takes one Metro employee to say yes to a loan, but two to say no. The bank has realized that not all valuables can be digitized, so Metro Bank offers safe-deposit boxes in all its stores, which are in such high demand that they basically pay the bank's rent on premium high street corners.

Iain Kirkpatrick, managing director of retail for Metro Bank, says: "We are a bank with an extreme focus on personal customer service and the communities we operate in. We have revolutionized personal banking at a time when everyone else talks about online banking, and our expansion with a new store every month shows that people appreciate the way we do business."

4

REDEFINE LOCAL IDENTITY

In a globalized and urbanized economy, we have to modernize the concepts of 'local' and 'community'. We are used to asking people where they are from and getting answers like "I'm Chinese," or "I'm from London," as if that made any real sense. There are 1.3 billion Chinese, and they are all different, and there are nine million people in London, some of whom are Chinese. As a matter of fact, 30% of all Londoners speak English with a foreign accent. And London isn't just London; it's split up into boroughs and neighbourhoods where people live in their own communities. The author, model and performer Taiye Selasi outright rejects the question: "Don't ask me where I am from – ask me where I feel local." She suggests we modernize and revitalize the terms 'local' and 'community'. The traditional way of defining people's origin and community has grown out of the Industrial Age and does not reflect the 21st century.

Selasi calls herself an Afropolitan; she is a young woman with African roots and with life experiences from the entire world. She has parents in Ghana and Nigeria, she was born in London, grew up in Boston and has lived in New York, New Delhi and Rome.

Selasi is a serial local who thinks that people define their identity based on the geographic and mental areas where they feel local and where they feel they belong. In a modern world where people and cultures constantly blend, the importance of our original countries and ethnicity is reduced. Not all of us live as exotically as Selasi, but we all know the feeling. We may have moved several times in our lives, maybe studied or worked in another city or even another country. Eventually we have a number of environments where we feel at home and feel we belong. Only a few people would put a single cross on a map; more likely we will draw a geographic pattern showing where we feel or have felt local.

This situation of 'serial localness' will inevitably grow in the coming years and challenge traditional understanding of local communities. Communities will be undergoing constant restructuring and subsequently will offer new opportunities to businesses that bother to understand these communities.

Selasi thinks that local identity should be interpreted and defined through three questions:

1. WHAT ARE YOUR *RITUALS*?

Which behaviours do you share with your community? Do you have the same football team, do you bike or drive to work, what do you eat and drink, and what cafés do you frequent?

2. WHO ARE YOUR *RELATIONS*?

Which flesh-and-blood people constitute your personal network, who are the people you often talk to and who are important in your life? Selasi does not talk about Facebook friends, but people you are emotionally and physically attached to in order to feel part of the community.

3. WHAT ARE YOUR *RESTRICTIONS*?

What limits your connectedness to your community? Are there any forms of discrimination, are there poor social and economic conditions that make it difficult to find a job, get a loan for your house or business, or get an education?

Based on the three-tier local definition of rituals-relations-restrictions, people and customers may well be next-door neighbours without really belonging to the same community. That's the case with immigrants who are badly integrated, for instance. But it's not just ethnicity and culture that may divide people: age and education may, as well. Comparing a 15-year-old GenZ with a 60-year-old baby boomer may be like comparing two different universes. It's not unheard of that young people leave a community because it doesn't offer job or education opportunities. **Restrictions** is the least exciting of the three **Rs**, but it often plays the dominant role in understanding communities.

Today, new communities and cultures emerge across traditional borders. This means that new markets are being redefined, and those companies and organizations that understand the new relations – and detect and identify the restrictions – may become the winners of the future.

5

NEO BANKS FOR NEW COMMUNITIES

Over the last five years, I have followed scores of young fintech start-ups and seen a new breed of financial institution come to life. What distinguishes these challenger banks – or neo banks – from the incumbents is basically their ability to identify new communities. The incumbent banks think in 'products and markets', whereas the young disruptors think in 'tribes'. Actually, they don't think of themselves as disrupters; it is the venture capitalists funding the star chasers who talk about disruption, not the start-ups. They are primarily interested in solving the financial restrictions that their community members experience.

The tribe or the new community that attracts the main attention of the challenger banks are the smartphone generation – the nomad tribe, the members of the gig economy. Young people are constantly on the move towards a new job or project, a new place to live or the next coffee shop where they can charge their mobile devices. They are the ones using Uber and Airbnb, in tight jeans, sneakers and t-shirts, and at least one tattoo.

The founders of the neo banks share the rituals of the people they want to help. They are neither white- nor blue-collar bankers – they are hoody bankers! Coconut is such a bank – or rather, a bank dream in the making. I have followed the project over the last couple of years from when the idea first hatched to now, with 20 employees and still a long way to go. The name itself shows a new approach to banking; it is intended to become a bank for freelancers. There are 1.7 million full-time freelancers in the UK alone, people who focus on finding work and doing it, and they do not care about bookkeeping and accounting – at best, they keep their receipts in a shoebox.

Founders Sam O'Connor and Adam Goodall know their tribe – they share information about their lives and business on every possible social media channel.

Another example of community banking is the London-based Revolut. The bank was founded by the Russian Nikolay Storonsky with the idea of removing the credit card fees that young people had to pay when they travelled the world. Why should Americans pay high exchange fees for using their card in Europe and vice versa? Why not let them clear the various currencies between each other? Revolut discovered a community before the incumbents did. Its staff were not bankers in suits and ties. They were young people in t-shirts and sneakers like their peers in the international youth community.

They shared relations and rituals, and they identified a restriction: moving money around freely. Today, Revolut is about far more than clearing fees on credit cards. It has become an international bank with two million users all over the world. It offers users access to free accounts in some 30 currencies and the ability to move their money freely between all these currencies at the interbank rate – that is, the same exchange rate that the banks are paying themselves.

As Storonsky says, "Our users are working in the gig economy. They may do a job for an American company one day and be paid in dollars and work for a German customer the next and send an invoice in Euros. We want to make this possible for them. Revolut spotted a new tribe that wasn't there when the traditional banks were founded 100 years ago and which have not yet gotten in sync with the relations, rituals and restrictions of the new community."

THERE IS MORE TO ECONOMY THAN MONEY

In 2017, at the 50th anniversary party of The Beatles' famous Sergeant Pepper record, Sir Paul McCartney was interviewed and asked why the band had created the iconic LP cover. Paul McCartney explained that when he was young and wanted to buy a record, he took the bus to a record shop in Liverpool called Lewis's and on his way back, on the top of the double-decker bus, and he unwrapped the new record and all the way home excitedly studied it.

McCartney's experience when buying music is far from our experience with music and video streaming. If we want to listen to a new artist or see a new film, we no longer need a couple of hours to obtain it. We have music and video *on demand.* Anything you want, you got it! But that hasn't made us any happier, has it? On the contrary, today we don't appreciate what we have in the way Paul McCartney did because of the abundance of opportunities and the speed at which we can access them.

I appreciate that there are advantages in getting what we want quickly. Waiting for a long time is not necessarily a good thing. But sometimes it is! Waiting and working for something can enhance our satisfaction. For Amazon and a lot of online shops, it's all about reducing the price and the time of delivery. It's not quite the same for Starbucks. It wants to keep the price up – and the costs down for the company – but like Amazon, the company is working extremely hard to reduce every aspect of waiting time. Customers can now order their coffee from an app on the way to the café, so it is ready for them when they enter the shop. Starbucks is constantly trying to shave off seconds of the payment process, too.

Why is that really so important when most of us sit in the coffee shop for half an hour or more? Starbucks could make the ordering and payment process more exciting – it could introduce a dating line in the shop instead. If you talked to the person in front of you, it might give you a free croissant for entertaining its guests! Everybody talks about the importance of networking, and making a new friend is more important than contactless payments.

The point is, when we talk about economy, we cut out the human factor. It's time and money. I definitely agree that we should not reject the possibility of making faster and cheaper payments, but when we design the future economy, we shouldn't ignore the fact that financial decisions are not only based on numbers. We overpay for the coffee in coffee shops – my grandfather would never have paid £4 for a latte, he would have considered that a waste of money. But it isn't to most of us. Coffee from a barista has become one of our rituals, something that defines us as part of a certain tribe.

And we are willing to stretch ourselves financially to become accepted members of preferred communities. People pay thousands for a Louis Vuitton bag, even though they can get a much bigger bag at a fraction of the price at Marks & Spencer.

Bankers have forgotten all that. They have their figures and algorithms, and they don't see their financial services as much more than just a money transaction. When you get a loan, the lender's decision to let you have the money is seldom based on a personal relationship. It's based on an algorithm fed with big data, and it doesn't help to smile to the banker. Banks have algorithms for assessing the statistical risk of not getting their money back. They think of customers as data.

They ignore the fact that most customers themselves think it is important to pay their debts, and that close personal relations between banks and customers increase loyalty between both parties. As Selasi said, "To build a strong community, you need people who matter to you more than Facebook friends."

6

MAKE IT NEW

I have worked closely with business executives in the financial industry since the financial crisis in 2008, and the phrase I have heard the most is, "We have to digitize." And when I don't look as if I agree, they add, "We have to innovate, too." I'm still not impressed. The entire financial market argues that the financial system and its institutions need to be modernized. But that will only turn them into smoother and more efficient versions of what they already are today. And that is not good enough if we want to have success in the 21st century.

For that purpose, we need true modernism! And to understand what that means I'd like to take those who create our economy back in time and introduce them to the critic and poet Ezra Pound (1885 – 1972) who, among others, was a mentor for Ernest Hemingway. I 'met' Ezra Pound in a second-hand bookshop in Southampton, where I stumbled across his essay collection, *Make It New*, published in 1934.

Today, his thoughts are more relevant than ever.

Make It New was the modernist war cry of Pound. He wanted poetry to change with the world around it – he wanted poets to experiment and take inspiration from life. He wanted writers to reinterpret the past and give it new forms that worked in modern time. It was all about creation and breaking existing forms whenever possible through the use of technology. Modernism was about finding everything that was holding progress back and changing it by making it new, by being as distinct and direct as possible. Hemingway listened to what Ezra Pound said. He developed his own modernist writing and cut down the amount of words to a minimum supported by the fact that, as a journalist, his manuscripts had to be wired from Europe to his editor at the *Toronto Star*, who had to pay the telegraph company per word. Make it short, make it new and Hemingway did it and got in sync with the modern industrial age, which made him one of the 20th century's leading writers.

We are in the exact same situation today as we were 100 years ago when the world experienced a host of new technologies and Ezra Pound wanted us to make a new world. We gave up horses and steam engines for cars, electricity, aircraft, wireless communications and boundless other technologies, which we used to build a new and modern society that was completely different from that of the 19th century. We really made everything new, as Ezra Pound demanded. We have taken society, as we know it, as far as the known technologies have allowed us to. Now a new set of technologies have emerged, such as smartphones, blockchain, solar panels and social media, and we have to find a way to apply them to a world that is new again.

Up till now, we have basically applied new technology to the old thinking and the old economy – we have digitized, but we haven't made our economy new. It's still industrial, and this is what we have to change in order to create real progress. To seek inspiration for that, we shouldn't go to management schools and consultancies. Ezra Pound warned us against that. Instead, we must leave our money towers in Manhattan and Canary Wharf and take inspiration from life on the street level.

CROWDFUNDING FOR COMMUNITIES

Four years ago, I interviewed a young woman, Cynthia Shanmugalingam, who had just set up the first food incubator in London, Kitchenette. A few years later, I came across one of her street kitchen projects on the crowdfunding site Spacehive, which specializes in projects "that make local places better". With the project, Shanmugalingam wanted to establish a fish and chips outlet that would serve healthier, more modern fish and chips in the borough of Tower Hamlets. It would hire local young people and train them to run the new street kitchen.

I love fish and chips and for fun I joined the project, investing £100, which would be paid back in fish and chips. They needed to raise £30,000 to get their shabby food truck renovated, and they eventually succeeded, thanks to the support of 187 backers, most of whom were more generous than me.

A few months later, I was invited to the launch of the Fish & Chips Kart in Dalston, East London. The young street-food enthusiasts were not ready when I arrived, so I invited one of the other micro-founders to a pint in the bar. We were offered a '40 FT' lager.

"I don't know this brand," I said.

"Oh, that's our local beer," the youth behind the bar said.

"Why the name 40 FT?"

"We make it in a 40-foot container down in the yard," he answered.

For the first time, I began to believe in local economy as a sustainable alternative to global branding. One in three people in Hackney lives in poverty and unemployment is high, but their beer and fish and chips are premium quality and, by making it locally, they take responsibility for their own future.

After I had eaten my fish and chips, I asked Shanmugalingam how many street kitchens she had helped to get on the road. **Her answer was eight!** This means that the number of young people she has helped to get up in the morning and provide on-the-job training for has to be counted in three figures. What puts Shanmugalingam's achievement in perspective is an interview I had with the CEO of a local Norwegian bank at about the same time Shanmugalingam founded her food incubator. The Norwegian bank had set up an incubator fund of £500,000 with the goal of supporting young start-ups in the bank's local community. I asked the bank's CEO how many businesses the bank had put on the road in the same three-year period. **His answer was one!** The reason for the meagre result, according to the CEO, was that the local Norwegian start-ups that had applied for investments hadn't been able to convince the bank that they could survive and repay their loan.

The question here is: who has the better business model – the bank or Shanmugalingam?

ACCELERATORS AND INCUBATORS OF STAR CHASERS!

Over the last ten years, we have seen a new type of *company factory* emerge like mushrooms all over the planet. They are called incubators or accelerators, and these start-up farms have been a successful breeding ground for business disruption after the financial crisis in 2008. They operate with the same principles as the talent-contest-style shows we see on television. The people behind the accelerators and incubators scan a large number of start-ups – often as many as a thousand – and out of this overwhelming talent pool some ten or so start-up teams with the brightest business ideas are chosen to participate in a three- to six-month development programme called a boot camp. The teams are paid a survival fee for the period – pizza money – while being whipped into shape by mentors and advisors. Their initial business ideas are honed into new disrupting business models, while their software is developed further into a beta stage. The new entrepreneurs are often young computer wizards who understand the potential of new technology so much better than the decision makers in big corporations who are struggling to keep their heads above water and adjust a reluctant organization to modern times.

When the initial accelerator programme is over, it's time for the new start-ups to pitch their businesses in front of a live audience of venture capitalists and business angels. On these demo days, there may be hundreds of investors who are willing to pay millions to get a share of the future success of the new wonderkids. It starts with modest seed investments, just to get the start-up team going, and then several funding rounds follow until hopefully the new venture can sail by its own steam.

Venture capitalists invest in start-ups only to exit again. That happens when the company gets listed on the stock exchange or someone from a competing business decides to buy its up-and-coming competitor while it still can. An accelerator such as RocketSpace in San Francisco, which also opened a co-working space in London, prides itself on having facilitated the creation of 19 unicorns since its launch in 2011 – among them formidable start-ups like Uber and Spotify that have shaken the taxi and music industries. Together they are worth $88 billion.

The founder of RocketSpace, Duncan Logan, says that his accelerator programme focuses entirely on the top 5% of already funded tech start-ups; the rest are rejected. The world's biggest tech accelerator, the Y Combinator, receives 6,000 applicants for each programme, of which 5,900 are filtered away. The aim for these modern business development centres is not helping start-ups with their dreams, it is to create gigantic profits for the investors who take the risks. That is what venture capitalism is all about, and it's nothing to get upset about. They lose a lot of money, too.

Over the last five years, I have followed a number of young start-ups and have been impressed with both their successes and those of the accelerators. When a young start-up is accepted into an accelerator programme, its chances of survival grow from maybe 5% to 80%, and it has an opportunity to grow exponentially. That's the whole idea. In just three years, the international challenger bank, Revolut, which started in the Level39 fintech accelerator programme in London in 2015, has raised $330 million in nine funding rounds and attracted more than two million users. It is now a unicorn worth $1.7 billion with plans of expanding globally.

Since the launch of the first accelerator, Y Combinator, in 2005, accelerator business has grown into a borderless industry. The latest Global Accelerator Report 2017 identified 1,500 accelerators around the world, of which it interviewed 570 that have funded a total of 11,000 start-ups and enabled them take the first step into the business world. The average seed funding is between $20,000 and $50,000 per start-up, and the norm for the accelerators is ten to 30 start-ups a year. The number of accelerators has surged in recent years, and we are still yet to see what happens in China, which, according to official numbers, now has some 7,500 incubators from which a stunning quarter of a million small enterprises have emerged. China wants to be the innovation country of the world and is aiming for 10,000 incubators and accelerators in 2020, with 100 of these overseas. The Chinese accelerator ambition is expected to generate three million jobs and 2,000 listed new companies. And they are all tech-driven.

There are numerous blurred lines when we talk about incubators and accelerators. An incubator tends to help start-ups at a very early stage, whereas an accelerator, as the word implies, helps the young company scale its business further. The key benefit of both 'start-up factories' is that they offer an ecosystem that brings together established corporations, investors, new talent and technology. Before accelerators, young entrepreneurs with fresh ideas and new technological insights had to bang on a lot of corporate doors to get support and investors, and corporations had difficulties finding talent. Now everybody meets on the accelerator platform.

For the support they give, accelerators tend to take two thirds of the start-up's equity, typically between 2% and 10%, but there is a trend towards other business models as the exits have been fewer than anticipated at the outset. Some accelerators have corporate sponsors; others are owned the big international companies. Many corporations have realized that it is difficult to develop new business models within their own organizations. Just think of companies such as Blockbuster, Kodak, Nokia and HMV that died in the process. The accelerators have become a driving force in the renewal of companies in the corporate rainforest. A fintech start-up like Transfer-Wise is up to eight times cheaper than traditional banks intransferring people's money abroad. This is why they are called disruptors. Long term, the incumbents don't stand a chance against the newcomers.

There are *three* major problems with the present accelerator model financed by venture funds:

First, the agenda is being set by young geeks on fixed-wheel bikes in Silicon Valley and Shoreditch. Second, they are backed by venture capitalists who are just waiting to cash in so they can invest their profits in yet another tech start-up that disrupts another existing industry. Third, most accelerators are focused on new technologies that turn jobs into software.

But what about all those people stuck in between the clever young start-ups and the super-rich tech investors? All the middle-aged men and women who are not change makers! All the people without a college education who cannot think up techy disruptive businesses! They are ignored in the Silicon Valley narrative, and if they want to open a café or a bicycle shop, there are no venture funds or banks to support them because they are not scalable. They will never become unicorns or get listed in the City.

We have put our future in the hands of two relatively small groups in society that can create a more efficient world that just doesn't need people. The new supermarket Amazon Go proudly announces that, thanks to smart technology, its new shop operates entirely without staff. The hedge fund Aidyia is like many other financial services based on AI and its founder, Ben Goertzel, optimistically claims: "If we all die, Aidyia will keep trading." Similarly, Uber and the other ride-hailing companies that are in the process of exchanging professional taxi drivers with amateurs are now trying to develop driverless taxis that will the amateurs from their jobs as well.

The *digitization of everything* is felt in local communities. Hundreds of shops are closing each week in the UK, and their windows are either left empty or are snapped up by national and international retail chains. In 2017, the number of closures in the UK was 5,855. The chairman of The Brixton Pound calls this development "blandification", as every high street now looks and feels identical with its Starbucks, Tesco and Boots. Shopping becomes boring and alienating. To stay competitive, supermarkets have introduced self-checkout service for their customers, which has led to those at the cash register losing their jobs – and the customers losing someone to talk to!

The present agenda for the future grows out of a global technology ecosystem that is creating a vicious circle for the Western world. The high-tech agenda doesn't have a sustainable vision. What will happen when these plans are realized? When we live in a jobless world run by algorithms, important decisions are made by our smart watches, connected to the global internet of things that will tell us when we have to go to the gym and when to order a vegan pizza, all without having to talk to any human beings?

Does this sound unrealistic? Well, it isn't. The Silicon Valley futurism is more or less a replica of the futurism that emerged in Italy in the 1920s. Futurism was an artistic and social movement that emphasized speed, technology, youth and violence, and objects such as the car, the aeroplane and the industrial city. Its front figure was the Italian philosopher Filippo Tommaso Marinetti, who talked about the beauty of war and created noisy music made from recordings of roaring cars, while filling the room with smoke that made his audience cough heavily.

That was his prediction for the 20th century, and he was horrifyingly accurate! Marinetti had the trends on his side and so does Silicon Valley today. I believe any future will be defined by the agenda and narrative told by the trendsetters, and right now Silicon Valley is doing all the talking.

But we shouldn't blame the tech companies. They are just the toolmakers, getting things to go their way simply because we are too lazy to dream new dreams ourselves. We need to write a new and even more exciting narrative that this time will involve the entire population.

It is people like Shanmugalingam with her food incubator who are writing the new narrative. She makes the local neighbourhood a better place to live. She creates jobs and serves better food for the rest of us. Not long ago, when I visited one of Kitchenette's street kitchens in Tower Hamlets, I learned that Europe's biggest fintech accelerator, Level39, was being closed and turned into a specialized co-working space instead. Its managing director told the press, "The accelerator idea is dead!" Obviously, because the investors could not exit their investments fast enough. That may be true from their perspective, but I disagree that the accelerator is dead. I think it is a formidable tool.

Level39 in London's new financial district is only a stone's throw away from where Shanmugalingam builds her street kitchens in a neighbourhood where many households have an annual income of less than £15,000 a year, whereas people working half a mile away in the money towers of Canary Wharf probably have an average annual income of £100,000. The problem for the business angels in Level39 is probably that they are too high up to know what matters on the street level.

There is a clear difference between the success factors for accelerators with scalable and un-scalable start-ups. Most tech start-ups take jobs away, whereas un-scalable start-ups such as hairdressers, hotdog stalls and bike workshops have to hire people when they become successful. This is why we need different models for funding labour-intensive businesses.

7

LET'S START WITH FOOD

In the global economy, the venture-fund-backed start-ups want to change the world from the top, whereas in the local economy the start-ups change the world from the bottom. And food seems to be the ideal starting point. In her book, *A Steak in the Economy*, Cynthia Shanmugalingam writes that a good place to eat makes a good place to live. Creative independent food outlets can change an area completely.

Brixton Village and Market Row are prime examples. In 2009, the owners of two forgotten and half-empty shopping arcades in Brixton in South London gave free leases to small units to encourage new businesses to move in. It was a bright idea, as the arcades became an incubator for scores of new restaurants offering food from all over the world. This has turned Brixton Village and Market Row into food meccas that attract people from across the whole city. One of the restaurants, Honest Burger, which started in Brixton Village in 2011, has since expanded and opened 25 restaurants across London, creating new jobs and better quality of life. Their idea was to create the best quality burger you could possibly get with British produce. From the outset, the founders bought their beef from the best butchers in London. Today they have their own butchery and buy their beef from small farmers in the Scottish Highlands from animals living outside, eating grass.

The lift that the restaurants provided for the arcades has rubbed off on the rest of the Brixton community, with a danger of gentrification. The property value of these arcades has surged, but until now the owners seem to have balanced the development well. All the original shops are still there – and there are no chains in sight.

Five years later, in 2014, Brixton did it again. On an empty building site, the Borough of Lambeth allowed the local community to open businesses in a new pop-up business centre built of shipping containers. Again, street food and beverages from all over the world were the means to growth and now, Pop Brixton attracts a million people a year. The businesses are all small and entrepreneurial, the set-up is cheap and without blandification. It really seems that reshaping an economy starts with the food. The former head of regeneration delivery for Hackney Council, Andrew Sissons, said in *A Steak in the Economy*: "Food is the cornerstone of our strategy for regeneration in the borough of Hackney."

Eating out is part of a modern lifestyle. American families spend more money on restaurants now than on groceries, not least thanks to the millennials – and the pattern is the same in the UK. Over the last ten years, the number of coffee shops in the UK has doubled. And, interestingly, independent cafés are growing as fast as Costa, Nero and the other chains. People want diversity when they look for a place to eat or get their next flat white. This willingness to spend money on artisan coffee and food has never been stronger and, at the same time, people are looking for creative places to go.

People like Shanmugalingam are really able to compete against opponents that are bigger and wealthier. Small street kitchens, creative cafés and restaurants have both time and millennials on their side; they are supported by the mega-trends.

More and more people want to become food entrepreneurs, and for many their future begins through food or kitchen ncubators. A report from Econsult Solutions, "US Kitchen Incubators: An Industry Snapshot", reveals that the number of kitchen incubators in the US doubled in just three years. There are now more than 200 incubators that support entrepreneurs who want to get into the food business, either by manufacturing their own products or opening a restaurant. In 2013, many critics said that kitchen incubators were just a post-recession fad that would peter out once the economy regained its footing. That hasn't been the case. On the contrary, young people's interest in starting their own food business has never been stronger. Consequently, so is the need for support and access to a professional ecosystem. Start-ups need both business and practical education; they need production facilities and business connections. All of this is provided by the incubators, and the report expects that the number of incubators will continue to grow for three reasons: there is an increasing demand for artisanal food, the sharing economy is gaining momentum and there is a spike in entrepreneurship as a career.

THE NEW START-UP CULTURE

When young people want to start a new street business, they don't go to the banks. First, because they expect to get a 'no', and this would probably be a sensible move by the bank, because restaurants of any kind are risky business. Second, banks and food trucks do not belong to the same urban culture. The people eating or starting street food are millennial nomads engaged in the gig economy. They don't take out a loan over five years to buy a food truck; they can't think five years ahead, so they go to the crowd to get their financial support, either their local community or their cultural tribe. It's a culture thing – a gigantic international bank doesn't fit into the street universe.

If you compare 'street food' and 'crowdfunding' on Google Trend, you'll see that they took off in public awareness more or less at the same time in 2011. They both grew out of the financial crisis and were simultaneously created by millennials with smartphones. We all get satisfaction from supporting a local business; we become owners and shareholders and develop personal ties with the business. We don't want to lose our money, but we don't see our involvement from a purely financial perspective. To participate in the creation of a business around the corner *makes us feel local* – we create new *relationships* and share *rituals.*

Crowdfunding is a new tool for financing new businesses. It's based on new technology, social media and creation of new communities. With crowdfunding and the growing trend towards new localism, we also see a new commercial alliance emerge between entrepreneurs, customers/founders and the municipalities. The latter have a vested interest in the new local business ventures that have a direct social impact on the community – and a number of local councils across the UK channel support to local projects through crowdfunding sites. And the opposite also takes place: 10% of UK's councils actually go to the crowd to get financial support for their projects.

Crowdfunding can offer equity or reward for its investors. The most famous reward-based crowdfunding site is Kickstarter, which has attracted almost $4 billion for 150,000 projects through its global community of 15 million backers. These are projects of unknown people with a good idea, ranging from getting a new bicycle lamp into production to book publishing to making a new indie film. The idea is that you present your project and your need for money on the website and, when you have sufficient funding, you start production. In other words, it's a completely different business model from what we are used to and it's less risky for everybody – except maybe the customers, but they are only investing a small amount. Crowdfunding is a key element in the sharing economy.

If the financial targets are reached, the projects go into production and the backers get a bicycle lamp, a book or a ticket to the film premiere – and maybe the chance to meet the director after the show or perhaps even to get a Tesla 3.

Crowdfunding sites have proven, powerful means of getting projects into production. The most successful has been the Pebble project, a smartwatch that was launched on Kickstarter in 2012 and through three campaigns received $45 million in funding from 200,000 backers, who all got a hip piece of wearable that clearly distinguished them from the mainstream iWatch tribe.

Crowdfunding is also changing the book publishing landscape. With almost 3,000 new titles each year, Kickstarter has won a seat among the top four publishing houses in America. It has its own publishing director and has funded 13,297 titles in nine years.

The other kind of crowdfunding is based on equity. Here the investor gets a share in the company and helps it get started or grow further. At the beginning of this book I mentioned an event in Shoreditch in London, where I met Darren Westlake, who told me about his new venture, Crowdcube, which aimed to help young companies raise money by offering investors equity. Since then, Crowdcube has achieved remarkable results. A few years after the event in Shoreditch, I started to see Crowdcube posters on the tube and adverts on the double-decker buses outside my window. Since its inception in 2011, Crowdcube has raised over £400 million for 650 successful projects and has become the leading equity-based crowdfunding site in the UK, followed by Seedrs. In 2017, the two sites together raised more than £250 million for start-ups and Crowdcube reveals one third of the investments were made directly from smartphones.

Compared to the £15 billion that was raised through IPOs on the London Stock Exchange in 2017, £250 million from equity crowdfunding may seem like a drop in the financial ocean. But it's not a relevant comparison – it's like comparing haute couture fashion with spring sales at Marks & Spencer. When times are changing – as they are right now – it is much more interesting to see what the outliers and trendsetters are doing than looking at both the early and late majorities.

And the newcomers are attracted to crowdfunding. Some of the most promising new challenger banks, Revolut and Monzo, sought new funding through equity-based crowdfunding in 2017. Revolut raised £5.3 million through Seedrs. More than 40,000 people wanted to invest in the company and the new banking app could have raised £18 million had it been allowed by legislation. Monzo was successful in raising £2.5 million from 6,800 small investors through Crowdcube in less than four hours.

It's interesting that these two new banks – founded five years after the financial crisis – not only represent a new business model for banking, but use a different model to funding themselves, too. We are indeed looking at the business catwalk of London, and it may be a valuable glimpse into the future.

Britain's most successful craft beer, BrewDog, is based on the same crowdfunded business model. The brewery was founded in 2007 in the town of Fraserburgh, north of Aberdeen in Scotland, by two men and a dog: James Watt, Martin Dickie and Bracken. BrewDog has since expanded with bars around the world, a new production brewery in America and another planned for Australia. In 2011, BrewDog started to finance its expansion through the crowdfunding programme 'Equity for Punks', which has raised £50 million from 75,000 "beer-loving investors". Today, BrewDog has a valuation of £1.7 billion and Crowdcube prides itself on the fact that the website has now been involved in the creation of the first crowd-funded unicorn. Crowdfunding has the same potential as venture capitalism.

According to a report from the crowdfunding site Fundly, crowdfunding raised more than $40 billion globally in 2017 and, if you include peer-to-peer lending, you may add a further $25 billion. Fundly predicts crowdfunding will be a $300 billion industry by 2025, but we don't know if that will prove to be the case and it's not really important.

James Watt describes BrewDog's business philosophy in the book, *Business for Punks: Break All the Rules – the BrewDog Way*, where he urges entrepreneurs to start a revolution. "Don't start a business, start a crusade! You need a reason to exist; it's not enough to start a company, start a revolution that will never die!" BrewDog is planning to have its own IPO in a couple of years and go live on the stock exchange, giving its thousands of small investors a chance to cash in. Let's hope it'll keep the revolution alive.

Since 2008, the number of craft breweries in both the UK and US has tripled, and their market share has doubled. This trend of small breweries winning market share is the same all over the world.

"Craft beer is leading the way in the surging popularity of artisan products and has pushed aside other brands in high street bars," said beer writer James Simmonds to the *Yorkshire Post.* "This increasing popularity has transformed many microbreweries into highly profitable businesses for entrepreneurs looking for a niche position in the food and drinks market."

The growing customer migration from huge international beer brands to small local craft beers worries the big beer companies, which have gone on a shopping spree among micro-breweries. Anheuser-Busch controls 30% of the global beer scene and bought crowdfunded Camden Town Brewery a few years back, which caused a stir among local beer fans. Carlsberg bought another local brewery, London Fields Brewery, which was going bankrupt because of the founder's tax fraud. A few years ago, two beer giants would probably have moved production of their new acquisitions to a giant brewhouse elsewhere, but Anheuser-Busch instead decided to invest £30 million into new brewing facilities in Enfield, just 20 minutes away, and Carlsberg promised to restore London Fields' original facilities under the old railway arches in Hackney.

Both companies were well aware that if they wanted to keep their customers, they had to adopt a local approach. As one beer aficionado said: “We hate the big beer brands, that’s why we buy local beer.”

But my book is not about breweries or kitchen incubators, it’s about establishing a new and modern economy for everyone and, in this context, is it exciting that a small brand can become global.

8

MILLENNIALS ARE LOOKING FOR MEANING

Old brands are heading for trouble with millennials. The world's biggest branding machine, Procter & Gamble, spends a stunning $7 billion on advertising each year. It ranked number 12 out of 149 organizations on the World Value Index in 2017, which measures the extent to which Americans are inspired by brands' missions and the extent to which that inspiration drives active support and purchase.

But Procter & Gamble is only ranked at number 12 when you speak to baby boomers! That is people older than 55. When you speak with millennials – those below 34 – the company comes out at number 103 on the list. This is a sign of a generational chasm, and the picture is the same with the majority of other established brands. They are performing badly in front of the millennials – the biggest generation ever in history, with an alleged buying power of $24 trillion.

Many old super brands favoured by the boomers were created through advertising in mass media, whereas the millennials get their information online and from social media – not from newspapers, magazines and television. This is reflected in the companies and organizations that millennials rate the highest: Twitter, Snapchat, PayPal, Spotify, Uber and Kickstarter – companies that are online and don't invest in traditional advertising.

"People's perception of the value of a brand is more important than ever," says Brian Hardwick from the advertising agency Enso, which led the research. "We were interested in how people perceive the impact of brands, and, if there is a gap between their impact and how people are perceiving it, whether there's an opportunity for brands to close that." One of the conclusions from the research is that young people are looking for *meaning* and have a personal ambition to change the world, while older generations have a more relaxed attitude. Another takeaway is that millennials are sceptical about big institutions!

A bank like Metro Bank spends practically no money on advertising; it relies on word-of-mouth marketing. If you treat your customers well, they become fans who will tell others of their good experience. Maybe traditional branding is dead. For a company like Procter & Gamble, it is necessary to spend $7 billion on marketing to build the brand – but if a company grows out of a community where everybody feels they have a stake in the company and support it, brands are created for free.

Stories are important and, sometimes, new stories are far more valuable than established brands. We live in a time of pop-up shops. Millennials are nomads in a gig economy – they don't stay in the same place as long as their parents did and don't expect their world to look the same. They are constantly making new connections, and many businesses behave like rock bands on tour.

According to Moore's Law, computer power doubles every two years. It accelerates, and six months in 2018 is equivalent to ten years in the 1990s. It's important that we let go of our old creations, make new ones and enjoy the process. It's like fashion – it changes constantly. If you ask a fashion designer if it's annoying to have to design a new collection soon after they present their current one, their answer will probably be, "On the contrary, that's the beauty of it. I enjoy creating something new."

A few years ago, during London Design Week, the architect Amanda Levete opened a pop-up restaurant in Soho called Tincan. The restaurant only served canned fish. Tins of fish and seafood were displayed in a 'museum-type vitrine' before being dished up to customers to eat straight out of the can. The restaurant needed no kitchen, little staff and was as cool as cool can be. It might have been a success on London's St James Street, but six months after opening the restaurant closed permanently and moved to New York. The famous Danish restaurant

Noma did the same thing – suddenly it closed down in Copenhagen and, like another rock band, moved the show to Tokyo.

That's where small communities have their big chance. They can move about freely in a changing world, whereas big corporations struggle with legacy systems. Look at the incumbent banks with tens of thousands of employees and gigantic organizations with branches and technology centres. Their biggest problem is not getting new ideas or starting new businesses – it's getting rid of the old ideas and the old businesses.

Big companies that used to be on the offensive are now on the defensive – they spend their creative energy protecting what they once created instead of designing something that is in sync with time. They lose the initiative – and when that happens, luck doesn't show up as often as before.

What the World Value Index reveals is true. The old brands don't work as they used to – they represent a time and a culture that the next generation wants to put behind them. I met a young entrepreneur, Cecilia Larsson, from Helsingborg in Sweden. She has a start-up called Rescued Fruits that makes juice and marmalade from the fruit that the local supermarkets can't sell. Larsson rescues the fruit from ending in the rubbish bin – hence the name – and employs young people who otherwise can't get a job. Among them are a couple of employees with autism who help sort the fruit – for most people a tedious task, but for these young people it's what they do best. Rescued Fruits was crowdfunded by 126 local backers on FundedByMe.

Local brands have a story to tell and are closely related to people in the community in a way that global brands can't match, even with billions of advertising dollars. This is why big companies can be pushed on the defensive by young, inexperienced entrepreneurs with a dream. For many millennials, it's so much cooler to drink a Rescued Fruits product with a sustainable business model.

9

BROOKLYNIFICATION

With new modern localism as an alternative to globalization, cities, town and neighbourhoods become the future brands that attract people and inspire business. The challenge is to create a tipping point for the local economy, and that doesn't happen by rebranding a town or a neighbourhood and believing that marketing alone can bring people into an area. It must come from inside, as was the case with the Brixton arcades and Pop Brixton. First, you have to develop local produces, businesses, cafés and shops, and when that is done people from the outside start to look at the area with fresh eyes. Because now it *is* a new area!

Some years ago I talked to Will Fulford, who owns Camden Lock, a market in London that attracts eight million visitors each year. I asked him about the secret behind the success of the market that his father leased and later bought in the 1970s. The area mainly consisted of old, worn-down industrial buildings and there was a plan to make it a motorway – that never happened.

"We started modestly, by inviting small businesses to open workshops, stalls and a few restaurants that would cover our monthly rent," said Fulford. "We wanted to be financially sustainable. We didn't have to become the roaring success that we eventually became. We'd put together our Camden Lock Manifesto, which guides our decisions on how to populate the space. Central to this is the dual goal of becoming relevant to our local residents and worker communities, and re-engaging with a wider London audience."

Dreams often start small and grow along the way.

Brooklyn – one of New York City's five boroughs – is an example of a neighbourhood that has developed its own identity since the financial crisis and become a super brand that attracts attention from people all over the world because it represents some distinct values. It's not America – it's not even New York – it's Brooklyn, different from any borough in the world.

Joey Dembs, when director of the New York marketing agency Flamingo, said in an article in *The Guardian*: "Brand Brooklyn's rise is a result of millennials rejecting the mainstream, corporate America they grew up with, spurred on by a backlash against Wall Street. The Brooklyn mentality stands for local – locally sourced products – and there is a smallness to everything, where you can trace products from creation to production."

The Brooklyn Chamber of Commerce has a certification programme, Brooklyn Made, that ensures that only products manufactured in the borough can use the name Brooklyn, which, according to *The Wall Street Journal*, represents the values 'honest', 'fresh' and 'local'. The ambition to be local pays off. Brooklyn – which was considered a second-rate neighbourhood a generation ago – now has the lowest unemployment rate since the start of the 1990s and a job creation rate that is three times higher than the rest of New York City.

This Brooklynification is a trend that runs across the US. Portland, Detroit and San Francisco are just a few examples of cities that protect their names with equal ferocity. The city of San Francisco is doing what it can to keep large-scale 'formula businesses', the chain stores, out of town. In some neighbourhoods, chain stores are not allowed to open. Consequently, San Francisco has more independent businesses and 60% fewer chains per capita than any other big American city. To open a chain store in the city, a formula business has to undergo an economic impact analysis – how many jobs do they create and what is their financial impact on the community? The chain store must benefit the community; otherwise, it doesn't get in. This policy works to promote commercial diversity and give citizens a stronger role in shaping their own neighbourhood.

THE BURLINGTON CASE

Building a strong local economy that will regenerate a city neighbourhood isn't an elusive and unrealistic dream. It is indeed a solid alternative to globalization, which was proven by Bernie Sanders, who fought against Hillary Clinton to become the Democratic presidential candidate in 2016. Before Sanders went to Washington, he was mayor of Burlington, Vermont, where in 1983 he and the town government decided to create their own local economy for some 40,000 citizens. At the time, unemployment was rising and the main high street had 14 empty shops, so the council decided to design a new development programme that would support local entrepreneurs and small 'mom-and-dad' shops, encourage employee ownership of local businesses and fight the entrance of 'big-box' shops. This was rather controversial at the time – on the edge of communism – but the council pulled it off and since then Burlington is considered to be one of the most successful small towns in America. Over 30 years, politicians, businesses and citizens of Burlington have created a robust and sustainable local economy that has proven to be able to resist even the toughest economic conditions, which was underlined during the financial crisis.

From 2008 to 2010, America lost 8.8 million jobs and five million families had to leave their homes. Worst hit was Detroit, which was completely dependent on one industry:

auto manufacturing. The city almost disintegrated with 30% unemployment. One in four houses were left empty and the average house price fell below $7,000. You could actually buy a home for less than a few thousand dollars – without anybody being able to do so.

But in Burlington, life went on as though nothing had happened. The local farmers sold their flour to the local bakeries, which sold their bread to local coffee shops and restaurants, which provided employment to the town's citizens. Families didn't have to leave their homes because of the financial crisis; the town maintained an employment rate among the top ten in the country and in 2011 Burlington was rated the happiest small city in the US.

It was the ideas and economic models from Burlington that almost made Bernie Sanders the Democrats' presidential candidate against Donald Trump – and it is exciting to imagine how the election debate between Sanders and Trump would have been. They were both outliers and against the status quo, but placed on each side of the political scale. It indicates which trends we can expect to grow in the future. Sanders, the former small-town mayor, wanted to strengthen local communities and split the big banks into smaller units in the biggest economy of the world. He failed, and the big companies still operate freely in a global economy. But almost getting elected reveals that under the surface grows a wish for a new economy.

Burlington's economic model is inspired by the writer and environmentalist, Bill McKibben, who wrote the book *Deep Economy*, in which he says: "For the first time in human history, 'more' is no longer synonymous with 'better' – indeed, for many of us, they have become almost opposites." McKibben demands a new economy that benefits the community, each individual and the global environment and is the kind of economy Burlington developed.

The former head of business development in Burlington, Bruce Seifert, describes in the book *Sustainable Communities* that it is not a question of doing a few things right. A sustainable local economy is built by hundreds of small initiatives that basically involve listening to what the citizens want – and then giving it to them. But there is a structure behind it all:

- **Political support**: From the very beginning, the council agreed that the regeneration programme needed strong and long-term political support so work would continue under changing political conditions. The overall goals were described in a strategic plan, "Jobs and People," which has been updated four times since then.

- **Localize and socialize**: The city council wanted to localize the economy by focusing on local entrepreneurs and businesses and encouraging employee ownership to create strong community engagement.

- **Sustainability**: Burlington's council wanted to create economic, social and physical sustainability and supported outdoor living, exercise, healthy food and a good public health service. In 2011, Burlington was rated the healthiest town in the US.

- **Food production**: Food in the US is transported on average 1,500 miles from where it is produced and manufactured to where it is eaten. Burlington made the decision to produce 10% of its own food, which resulted in 100 new jobs and a healthier population.

- **Inclusion**: Nobody was to be kept outside the local economic growth and every time the council identified groups in trouble, they started new programmes that would help – for example, projects to support women in starting their own businesses or refugees in getting jobs.

- **Financing and funding**: Burlington realized that jobs that disappear are often better paid than new jobs created by entrepreneurs. Therefore, the town council created a number of investment initiatives that help finance both start-ups and existing businesses to grow.

Realization of the programme "Jobs and People" builds on a broad collaboration between private and public companies, civic organizations and citizens of the town, as it is taken for granted that everybody has a mutual interest in developing the town economy. This has turned Burlington into a business incubator with participation from everybody.

10

THE LOCAL MULTIPLIER FACTOR

There is a good reason why Burlington, Brixton, Bristol and hundreds of other cities want to develop a local economy. An endless number of research reports all confirm that if you shop locally, the money will circulate longer in your area.

If you spend £100 in a local shop, £45 will stay in the area, whereas if you spend the same amount in a national or international supermarket chain, only £15 remains. If you go out and eat in a chain restaurant, 30% of the money on the bill will stay local as wages to the employees. On the other hand, if the restaurant is local, up to 80% will remain, particularly if the restaurant buys its ingredients locally. Similarly, the restaurant will create two to three times more jobs than an international chain.

Research from the Institute for Local Self-Reliance shows that Amazon needs 14 people to create $10 million in revenues, whereas the average high street shop employs 47 people each time it makes $10 million in sales. If you look at independent shops, they employ 57 people to create these revenues. Local shops simply don't create the same economies of scale as online shops or chains, but they hire people – and I like people better than touchscreens. And when the owner of the shop makes a profit, they normally invest it in their community, as opposed to online shops. If you buy something on the internet, *all* the money you pay will most likely disappear from the community – unless the deliveryman from UPS is local – and if you buy from an international website such as Amazon and pay with PayPal, your money will probably even leave the country to be invested elsewhere.

And this hurts not just local commerce – it hurts the entire local infrastructure. When I was a young journalist at a local newspaper, we used to say that the price of the newspaper covered the content and the ads paid for printing and distribution. Now people don't read as many papers and magazines as before and those publications that survived don't have as many ads. The audience has gone online to social media, which now attracts a growing share of the marketing money. And this money leaves the local economy as well.

In April 2018, Mark Zuckerberg participated in a Congressional hearing in Washington, during which Utah's Senator Orrin Hatch asked: "How does Facebook sustain a business model in which users don't pay for your service?"

Zuckerberg was obviously taken aback by the question: how could US lawmakers be so ignorant? Then Zuckerberg blinked and said simply: "Senator, we run ads."

"I see. That's great." Hatch responded.

And that was the end of the senator's curiosity, which has since been ridiculed. But he might have pursued the question further: "How much money do you earn from these ads and where does this money come from?"

The answers would have been, "More than $40 billion a year – and our revenues are growing", and, "We get the money from advertising budgets that used to be spent on traditional mass media." Social media affects the local economy the same way online shopping does.

This is why the small town of Burlington and the big city of San Francisco try to keep the chains out of their local high streets. The argument that big-box stores and formula businesses ensure cheaper goods the consumers is rejected by *new economists* who claim that, in the long term, citizens are far better off with local shops. On top of that, we have the blandification that comes with the chains. Almost identical shopping centres and high streets give people a deja-vu feeling: "Haven't I been here before?" Life disappears from the streets and town centres, and there is no diversity because only chains with economies of scale survive.

11

NEW LOCAL CURRENCIES

In 2009, a think tank suggested that the Brixton neighbourhood develop its own currency and start to print its own money. This was a reaction to the financial crisis, with the intention being to take control of the local economy and not park the responsibility with the huge international banks. The result was the Brixton Pound – it has an equivalent value to a normal pound sterling, and is accepted as an additional currency in 250 local shops. At the moment, there is one million Brixton Pound in circulation and it will probably circulate forever – opposed to a pound sterling, where only 15 pence will remain in Brixton when it is spent in the local Tesco, for instance.

The Brixton Pound has had little effect on the local economy, perhaps due to a lack of marketing by the organization behind it, which is driven by volunteers. But it has had a strong impact as a 'social currency'. It's a powerful message in the community – we have our own currency, our own identity – with David Bowie on the Brixton ten-pound note. After his death, the Brixton tenner was sold on e-Bay for four times the denominated value.

The city of Bristol has similarly created its own currency, which has had a greater impact. At its launch in 2012, Mayor George Ferguson announced he would receive his salary in Bristol Pound, which is a viable payment for buses, local taxes and utility bills. As many as 800 shops in Bristol accept the local currency and the city's approach to local economy is very similar to that of Bernie Sanders' Burlington, which for a number of years also had its own currency, Burlington Bread, until it had to give in again to real dollars.

Bristol wants to create a sustainable economy in every sense of the word and has, among other initiatives, set up a food club, Real Economy, which collaborates with local food producers and creates a platform through which families and public institutions can buy and eat healthy local produce.

The Bristol Pound was created in collaboration with Bristol Credit Union, which is a local organization founded in 2005. It's not supposed to make a profit and has given 5,000 families living and working in the Bristol area access to affordable loans. Bristol Credit Union is one of the few financial institutions that actually operates according to the business model demanded by many new economists.

There are local currencies everywhere – in Totnes in Devon, Nantes in France, Berkshire County in Massachusetts.

A few years ago, the new Mayor of Barcelona, Ada Colau, expressed the idea that her city should have its own currency, and she immediately won support from her colleague in Valencia, Joan Ribó, who wanted one as well. And cities do it for the same reason: they want to keep money in their communities and improve the opportunities for small local businesses to compete against multinational companies.

NEXT-GENERATION LOCAL CURRENCIES

I love the colourful notes of local currencies, and I think they are useful in making the new economy visible. But as a means for local businesses to compete against big banks, cool fintech start-ups and powerful retail chains, local paper money is too laborious. We don't want to turn back time and re-establish a financial infrastructure that became obsolete ten years ago. We need to create a new and modern alternative that has time on its side and is even better than what exists today. And some of these alternatives are beginning to pop up. There are tech start-ups that are working on third- or fourth-generation local currencies, and they have some really cool models based on blockchain and crypto currencies, which in contrast to paper money is a 21st century technology.

Blockchain is the technology behind Bitcoin, which in itself is enough to create a substantial amount of scepticism from the business establishment. Blockchain is a technology where everybody involved in a business system has equal access to all information. That's not the case with our present financial infrastructure, where we need intermediaries like banks, payment providers and insurance companies to supervise the flow of money and values. But, if we put our business on a blockchain, we can trust information and transfer values safely between users.

When a group of people or businesses create a system based on blockchain technology, they need a common currency that all users accept – this is called a token, but is normally given a specific name. The first tokens established in 2009 were Bitcoins, and since then thousands of crypto currencies have been issued. It has become fashionable to fund the development of a blockchain-based business by selling the new tokens. It's called an initial coin offering or an ICO, which resembles an initial public offering or an IPO. It's about financing a business and, in an ICO, the people who buy the new crypto currency get a share of the future turnover on the blockchain model. One may call it a new form of crowdfunding based on blockchain technology and digital currencies.

In a digital world that is becoming increasingly connected, blockchain technology seems to be an ideal tool if you want to create a new financial infrastructure, and this is exactly what the Israeli start-up Colu has done. It has created a new-generation local currency that may be described as a 'flat-pack local economy' or 'a local economy in a box' and is behind four local currencies in East London, Liverpool, Haifa and Tel Aviv.

Colu's blockchain not only serves as currency for the local business community; it is a complete payment and marketing platform that enables local shops and businesses to build relations with their customers. It's a millennial lifestyle app put on top of the Google map, and all payments are done from a smartphone and in the local currency as, for instance, the East London Pound.

Users have to top-up from the outside economy – and the exchange rate is normally 1:1, but often users are offered incentives and get a meal cheaper if they pay with the local currency or they get a better exchange rate "because it's nearly the weekend"– or you may get paid from someone in the local currency. You can exchange your local digital currencies back again to the official currency any time you want.

I think the Colu currency is interesting for two reasons. First, it's a next-generation local currency that is based on brand-new technology ahead of the traditional financial infrastructure. Second, it can open a new generation of local economies in the coming years. At present, it creates the foundation for four different local currencies, but these four local economies are connected by a mutual digital currency reserve and there is a technical platform that makes it possible for these and other future local economies to trade with each other.

Every model we have seen so far with regard to local economy is some kind of protectionism, where the founders try to isolate the community from its surroundings. But with a mutual economic infrastructure like the one Colu provides, local communities have for the first time the opportunity to cooperate across borders and create a common distributed economy that will look a lot like the structures we see on social media. That gives new economy a better future. It becomes democratic as every community gets much more influence over – and responsibility for – its own economy.

12

SMALL IS BEAUTIFUL

There aren't many people today who know about the German-English economist Ernst Friedrich Schumacher, who died at the age of 66 in 1977. He is the man who coined the expression "small is beautiful" when he wrote the book of the same title with the subtitle: *A Study of Economics as if People Mattered.* It's a collection of essays that question the way we handle the economy and societies development.

Schumacher has become my hero and I think that his ideas and philosophy about people and the economy are even more relevant now than when they were created, spoken and written more than 40 years ago. During the energy crisis in 1973, and at the start of modern globalization, he was one of the first economists to question the mantra that 'big is better'. He was considered among the top 100 global thinkers and influencers of his time, more than four million copies of his book were published and he was invited to meet President Jimmy Carter in the White House.

Schumacher claimed that the modern economy wasn't sustainable and that we had to think of future generations, not spend all natural resources at once, and think of the planet. He considered 'gross domestic product' irrelevant in the long term because natural resources are limited and there are limits on how much pollution the earth can stand. Today, when climate change is on top of the global agenda, we have to admit that Schumacher's predictions were right 40 years ago.

He considered economy to be a tool to provide a better life for people and not a goal in itself. He thought that people were born to work because we have a splendid head and two wonderful hands that are able to create magnificent things. But it wasn't any kind of work: "Soul-destroying, meaningless, mechanical, monotonous, moronic work is an insult to human nature, which must necessarily and inevitably produce either escapism or aggression, and that no amount of 'bread and circuses' can compensate for the damage done."

Schumacher's most famous quote is probably this, which encompasses his philosophy: "Any intelligent fool can make things bigger, more complex and more violent. It takes a touch of genius – and a lot of courage – to move in the opposite direction."

With size follows heavier consequences of our mistakes, and I'm convinced that if Schumacher had been alive during the financial crisis in 2008, he would have suggested that our banks, businesses and systems be divided into smaller entities. This is what Bernie Sanders said.

In one of his essays, "A Question of Size", Schumacher wrote that when our cities get bigger than half a million people, they start to become less efficient. This is why it's important for organizations, cities, countries and corporations to rediscover their 'smallness'. I thought of Schumacher and his claim that there is a limit to when increased size results in increased efficiency; that was during the European Football Championship, when the Icelandic team got all the way to the quarter finals and beat England on their way. Iceland has only 330,000 people, but the country can match the best nations in the world in football and handball. And they amazingly qualified for the World Cup in 2018 too. It may be a coincidence, but most of London's 29 boroughs are home to 300,000 people. Is 300,000 people a magic size that provides you with all the talent you need to develop a sustainable community? Iceland functions well as an independent country; it has its own language, university and culture, and it worked itself out of a depression in 2008 without help from the outside.

The fundamental idea in Schumacher's economy is "lots and lots of small autonomous units" – this idea got a lot of attention for a few years before it slid into oblivion when Schumacher died.

I worked in the computer industry in the 1980s when computer power was doubling every 12 months, and everybody talked about how they now could create still more powerful and bigger mainframe computers with dumb terminals. Steve Jobs from the new company (at the time) Apple had a different view on this. He believed that still cheaper computer power should be distributed to everybody, not centralized, and his idea about a personal computer changed the world. When everybody thought that having a laptop computer was as far as we could bring it, Steve Jobs did it again when he launched the iPhone in 2007, again based on the idea of "lots and lots of small autonomous units."

I believe the world is ready to accept that *small is indeed beautiful* once more. Never has this idea been more relevant or realistic because, since the 1970s, we have created a new global communication infrastructure, not just an internet of computers, a mobile network of smartphones and a social media network for people, but soon also an internet of things that will serve as a platform for the fourth industrial revolution. This new infrastructure enables any of us to form infinite borderless organizations without a start or an end as networks and not the obsolete hierarchies that grew out of the 20th century industrial thinking.

Schumacher was certainly ahead of his time. In *Small is Beautiful*, he wrote: "I was brought up on the theory of 'economies of scale' – that with industries and firms, just as with nations, there is an irresistible trend dictated by modern technology for units to become ever bigger. It is quite true today that there are larger organizations than ever, but in Britain and the United States the number of small units is also growing, and many of them are also highly prosperous and provide society with most of the really fruitful new developments."

This was written 45 years ago, but could just as easily have been written today. As a matter of fact, it was re-written and updated in 2018 by the author and consultant Hermant Taneja, who coined a new post-industrial term, 'economies-of-unscale', in his book *Unscaled*. Since Henry Ford decided that we could have his cars in any colour we wanted as long as we chose black, big companies have had a competitive edge over small firms. Taneja questions this and claims that not only is size no longer an advantage, it is increasingly a disadvantage.

Over the last decade, we have talked a lot about *disruption*, so we already know how new, smaller companies are threatening the big established ones. But now Taneja stresses that they are in trouble explicitly because of their size.

In a report, "Disrupting Procter & Gamble", the research company CB Insights shows how, brand by brand, start-ups suck revenue and market share out of the consumer goods giant that has annual revenues of $38 billion. The young nimble competitors don't attack Procter & Gamble head on; if they did that they would lose to a giant that can afford to spend $8 billion on marketing. Instead, each one singles out one of Procter & Gamble's hundreds of brands that they can produce, develop and market better because they are closer to the consumers. How close can you be to millions of customers when you are in Cincinnati, in the middle of the US, and have revenues the size of Lithuania's gross national product?

The big banks are similarly threatened by *economies of unscale*. They have built gigantic empires with thousands of branches, tens of thousands of employees and enormous legacy computer systems developed before anybody had heard of Nokia mobiles. When small challenger banks that only exist on the screens of the customers' mobiles then attack the incumbent banks and take segments of dissatisfied customers away, then economy of scale suddenly becomes a problem for the incumbents. But how can small ventures with few resources suddenly threaten the established giants? This has been affected by two things: the emergence of new technologies and the new platform economy.

The British challenger bank Starling is an interesting case of economies of unscale. Within four years, entrepreneur-banker Anne Boden created a new bank from scratch, and its core banking system and most of its software are in the cloud with Amazon Web Services. The new bank is not burdened by legacy systems and hasn't had an expensive start-up investment.

One of its executives told me that Starling had a visit from the British Financial Conduct Authority, wanting to inspect the security and see the servers, which it obliged to according to rules of compliance.

"We don't have servers; why don't you ask Amazon? I think they have them in Ireland." How can an established bank with its own expensive datacentre compete against this? And Starling is not the only bank of this type. At a press meeting recently, another UK challenger bank, Redwood, explained how in just six months it had built its new bank system entirely in Microsoft Azure.

But the neo banks are not the only cloud-based economies-of-unscale businesses. If you wonder how Netflix is able to stream films to 125 million people around the world – and add some 25 million new users each year –

the answer is the same: Amazon Web Services! You no longer need your IT organization to do IT. If you have a bright business idea, you can buy production facilities as a service and compete against anybody within six months.

And economy of unscale works in all sizes and shapes. If you want to publish a book, you don't need a printing machine or a publishing company. You can buy everything in the value chain online as a service and publish books, films and music. And if you don't have the money, you can find that on the net, too, on crowdfunding sites.

We see the same business model in the manufacturing industry. A good example is Local Motors in Arizona, which employs 250 people but remains small enough to challenge companies like General Motors. Local Motors is based on 3D printing. It doesn't have its own designers but is dependent on freelance engineers and designers – and it doesn't have a big manufacturing plant, it sets up micro-factories. So, new technology enables small local companies to produce premium goods often at better quality than big competitors in economy-of-scale mode.

The same thing goes with food production. I learned about a company called Growing Underground that had taken a Second World War bomb shelter 100 feet underground in Clapham in South London and turned it into a greenhouse powered by LED light. Deep underground in 65,000 square feet of tunnels, founders Steven Dring and Richard Ballard grow pea shoots, red basil, rocket, coriander and many other herbs and vegetables without the use of pesticides and 100-odd times more efficiently than in a field. The business is booming and its produce is sold to supermarkets and local restaurants. In the US, food is transported 1,500 miles from farmers to consumers. Here they grow it in the middle of the city. Growing Underground has just 12 employees but is planning to expand soon with a second site under Clapham Common.

Regardless of its size, Growing Underground can compete with anyone. Like BrewDog and Monzo, it was also crowdfunded by Crowdcube. And I think it is about to. The big consumer brands don't lose ground to each other, they lose market share to the unscaled local businesses.

At the same time as small firms get access to scalable production facilities, they get access to platforms. Recently, I saw a Facebook advert at Charing Cross station in London. It was about a young designer with a small company in East London, Goodordering – crowdfunded, of course. The designer explained how she had opened an online shop in Seoul in South Korea through Facebook (that wants to grow its stake in the platform economy, too). Just ten years ago this would have been impossible for a small designer, but now anybody with a dream can do it thanks to economies of unscale. Whether you have a vacant room, a free car, some goods or services to sell, there is an Airbnb, a Lyft or an Alibaba for it all.

It's interesting to see how economies of scale companies react to the economies of unscale economy. Anheuser-Busch is on a craft beer shopping spree around the world. It has bought ten small craft breweries in the US recently and is constantly looking for small beer companies to buy in Europe and Asia, obviously because the giant is not able to create its own local brands. But each time it buys one craft brewery, ten new ones emerge.

General Electric (GE) is trying to create its own economies-of-unscale model with regard to talent support. The industrial giant has realized that despite its size, there is still more talent outside GE than inside, and the corporation has created a community called Fuse, which is a platform for bright brains who are not on the GE payroll but who can be insourced when needed. The Fuse community convenes entrepreneurs, scientists, coders, engineers and makers from around the world to solve product development challenges that General Electric cannot solve itself. Interestingly, the platform is developed in collaboration with Local Motors, which more or less invented the modern unscaled industrial business model.

13

THE EMPIRE STRIKES BACK – ACROSS THE GAP!

As mentioned previously, I believe that the launch of the iPhone made a chink in the global business surface in 2007. We all focused on the Lehman Brothers crash that year, but the important change was the smartphone. It changed the way we think, learn, seek information, buy, connect with each other and find our way in the globalized world. Today the crack has developed into a gap – for some a chasm – and the world is divided into two different game boards: the old one with its familiar rules and the new one with its rules devised by Silicon Valley.

I think that most people and organizations are well aware of whether they are on the new or the old game board. If they are on the old game board, they are out of sync and, if they don't do anything about it, they will shrink and eventually disappear. A lot of business and community leaders respond to the challenge by saying, "We have to digitize!" To be honest – they don't get it. It is not just about digitizing, it's about understanding the rules of the game on the new board and responding in a way that people and markets appreciate. It's normally technology that changes the world. It was the smartphone that turned the world upside down a decade ago, and I suspect the blockchain technology will do the same. Each time we experience a new game-changing technology, we are confronted with the question: How do we cross the gap and become successful players on the new pitch?

It can be done – and the Swiss watch industry has showed us how. Swiss watchmakers have excelled for centuries as masters of precision, until the mid-1970s when Japanese £20 digital wristwatches suddenly made even the most expensive Rolex ridiculously imprecise. It became known as the quartz crisis and in 1983 two thirds of all jobs in the Swiss watch industry had disappeared. Today, Switzerland is back as the global leader in time keeping.

How can that be?

Assistant Professor of Business Administration at Harvard Business School, Ryan L. Raffaelli, set out to find an answer. "It's possible to prolong the life of some technologies along with the organizations and communities that support them," he said, "and successful companies may be able to reposition a 'dying' technology by redefining its identity and value for the customers."

Swiss watchmakers could no longer use time-keeping precision as their main selling point. The new tech companies like Casio with their digital watches were better and cheaper at that. Then, according to Raffaelli, a Swiss management consultant named Nicolas Hayek started to buy up suffering Swiss brands and watch companies and consolidate them into the concern Société Suisse de Microélectronique et d'Horlogerie or SMH. He found some talented young designers and engineers and, in 1983, launched Swatch, producing colourful cheap electronic watches that were meant as a fashion accessory. Now the values were no longer precision or mechanical quality; it was all about fashion and Swatch became a roaring success with revenues that grew to 8 billion Swiss Francs in 2012.

But Hayek and the Swiss watchmakers didn't stop there. The old expensive mechanical watches that people had worshipped for centuries were rebranded, too. This time, branding values were not just about precision but identity, lifestyle and tradition. The message was now expensive mechanical watches that represented a centuries-old tradition and craftsmanship that would never go away. Look at more than 20 years of brilliant advertising from Patek Philippe under the slogan: "You never actually own a Patek Philippe. You merely look after it for the next generation."

What tech company can beat that? Yes, you may have the latest digital technology, but we own the history, my young friend. We've made watches for almost two centuries and when your technology becomes obsolete, our watches will still be ticking. This story of the Swiss watch industry is encouraging. It shows that you don't have to digitize mindlessly but may get across the gap on your own terms if you are willing and able to reposition.

In 2018 Ryan Raffaelli excelled again with a new report about another dying industry that had re-invented itself: the independent bookstores in the US. In the 1970s, most bookshops were independent; then came the mall chains and the big-box stores like Barnes & Noble that expanded across the US with their cheap books, cafés and deep couches. When everybody thought it couldn't get any worse for the independent bookshops, Amazon opened its business in 1995. The number of independent booksellers dropped 43% over the next five years, and in 2005 Amazon was ready to give the small shops the *coup de grâce* when it introduced e-books and Kindle. As one editor noted, "We expect print books to go out of print." But Amazon didn't make life miserable for just the independent bookstores. It threatened the big book chains, too, and in 2010 Borders went bankrupt and had to close 511 superstores with almost 20,000 employees across the US.

Then something happened.

"Independent booksellers started to bounce back," Ryan Raffaelli writes in his report, "Reframing Collective Identity in Response to Multiple Technological Discontinuities: The Novel Resurgence of Independent Bookstores". "Between 2009 and 2015, the American Booksellers Association (ABA) reported a 35% growth in the number of independent bookstores across the county, rising from 1,651 to 2,227 respectively and, at their annual conference, the ABA's CEO Oren Teicher opened his annual address by stating: 'It is a great time for indie bookstores. Bigger is not always better. We've shown it's possible to change and adapt. We've redefined who we are.'"

What did the independent bookshops do to change their future? Raffaelli's research offers three key findings:

- **Community**: The bookshops grew the idea of localism; they stressed the importance of consumers supporting their local communities by shopping locally. They won customers back from Amazon and other big players, not by lowering prices but by strengthening their connection to community values.

- **Curation**: Independent booksellers began to focus on curating inventory that allowed them to provide a more personal and specialized customer experience.

Rather than just recommending bestsellers, they developed personal relationships with customers by helping them discover up-and-coming authors and unexpected titles.

- **Convening**: Independent booksellers also started to promote their stores as intellectual centres for convening customers with likeminded interests – offering lectures, book signings, game nights, children's story times, young adult reading groups, even birthday parties. Some bookstores now host over 500 events a year that bring people together.

While all this happened, the American Booksellers Association (ABA) served as a glue to bind likeminded players together, facilitating partnerships between bookstores and other local businesses. The ABA also strengthened the collective identity of indie bookstores by helping its members share best practices, such as how to use social media to promote special events.

"The theoretical and managerial lessons we can learn from independent bookstores have implications for a wide array of traditional brick-and-mortar businesses facing technological change," Raffaelli says. "But this has been an especially fascinating industry to study because indie booksellers provide us with a story of hope."

The lesson from the Swiss watch industry is about globalization and the lesson from the American independent bookshops is about localization, but they both address the Silicon Valley challenge: existing businesses need to reinterpret themselves and become as relevant to consumers as they once were. It's also a lesson in economies of unscale. Amazon pressed Borders with 500 super shops out of business in 2011, but more than 500 independent and *unscaled* new bookshops emerged in their stead.

14

SMALL DATA AND HUMAN INTELLIGENCE

The interest in *big data* and *artificial intelligence* (AI) is overwhelming in the banking world right now, but will machine learning and data from the past save the financial services industry from disruption and bring better service to millions of people who feel they are not being served well at the moment?

The financial services industry is surrounding itself with an exponentially growing sea of data measured in zettabytes – that's terabytes with an additional nine zeros. This doesn't help banks under pressure in itself but, if you add new financial technologies such as big data and AI, experts believe that financial institutions will be able to get a better understanding of what goes on, make smarter decisions and design new tailored services for their customers. IBM talks about the future cognitive bank, where the ability to decode the data stream into information will transform the industry, and Accenture talks about the big data revolution that will bring new profitable growth to the sector.

Few disagree with these predictions, and all the big banks and technology companies subsequently pour tons of money into fintech start-ups working with new solutions based on big data and AI.

Successful hedge funds are now entirely based on AI. Capital markets are different from consumer banking, but it's generally the same everywhere. It's an algorithm that decides whether I get my loan or not, it's an algorithm from Marks & Spencer that has chased me through the internet since my Christmas shopping, and it will be algorithms supported by big data and AI that control future banking services.

To be honest, I think AI and big data are overrated. It's about time banking started to make human intelligence and small data a priority.

I'm supported in this line of thinking by the branding expert Martin Lindstrom. In his book *Small Data*, he writes that corporate decision makers are far too focused on finding the answers to their problems in big data from the past. Instead, he suggests they look at the way people behave in everyday life. All the little things people do give you a far better understanding of their behaviour and future needs. Lindstrom mentions that the late founder of IKEA, Ingvar Kamprad, made most of his strategic decisions based on what he learned from watching and talking to customers in the checkout queues. This is what Lindstrom means by small data.

When so many banks are exposed to disruption, it's more likely because they neglect the small data than because of big data. Let me give you a couple of examples. The online payment service Dwolla was founded in 2009 by Ben Milne, because he had a company selling speakers and was annoyed about paying 4% of his revenues in fees to credit card companies. The Revolut app was started by Nikolay Storonsky for more or less the same reason. Simple in the US was founded by Josh Reich because he felt that traditional banks were so complicated. Sam O'Connor, one of the two founders of Coconut, who plans to launch the first online bank for freelancers, said, "We have talked to a lot of freelancers, we know what goes on in their minds and what it takes for a bank to help them."

Getting a new idea and changing course is not about big data. Despite their fine equipment, I'm sure meteorologists sometimes look out the window to see what the weather is like, and we forgot to do just that in the run-up to Brexit and the presidential election in the US. Brexit and Trump came as surprises to most of us, despite all our data and algorithms. I think it's time community banks also start to look for small data and care more about what happens on street level.

Of course, I know that we will see more of big data and AI in the future. But while the capital market is trading by itself supported by robo-advisors, and the autonomous cars are driving around cities with robots on their way to work, and Marks & Spencer takes care of my Christmas shopping far better than I'll ever be able to do myself, I'll sneak out of the online world with my hard-earned cash and put it into a bank where management has human intelligence and can interpret all the small data I reveal when I talk about my trivial problems and my big dreams.

MILLENNIAL ECONOMY CREATORS AND MUTANT BANK KILLERS

If you want to predict the future, I believe there are two rules you have to take into consideration:

1. Don't ask the incumbent generation what it thinks is going to happen because it has no idea.

2. Don't overrate the short-term effect of new trends but never underrate the long-term effect.

Readers from Generation X, those above 35, may remember Shawn Fanning. He was the inventor of Napster, the legendary peer-to-peer file-sharing programme that enabled millions of people to share their music for free.

Corporate lawyers successfully stopped Napster in 2001, and rightly so because the music-sharing programme was basically facilitating theft of music from artists and the entertainment industry. But what the lawyers couldn't stop was the new digital technology that enabled free online distribution of entertainment. Yet, it took more than a decade before the new digital technology finally broke through and made online streaming mainstream.

It was Generation X that brought down HMV, Blockbuster and Kodak, and it was the oldest members of the succeeding Generation Y – the millennials – that delivered the *coup de grâce* and paved the way for Netflix, HBO, Instagram and iTunes and eventually Spotify, which disrupted iTunes and became the new format for buying music.

But it won't be Generation X or the millennials above 30 who will define the future economy. That will be the young millennials and Generation Z – the mutants – the 24/7 online generation, born with a smartphone with a broken screen in their left hand from which they communicate via social media their parents have never heard of.

The same was said about all the internet businesses before the dotcom bubble in 2001. I was there when investors lost faith in all the new ideas; but history has shown that the ideas were all right. Just ask Amazon or Alibaba. The investors and analysts simply forgot that it often takes a generation or two for new technologies to break through; there is a resistance in most markets because people need time to adopt and change habits, and normally the younger generation become the early adopters because they don't have habits to break or attitudes to change.

Shawn Fanning launched a new business model that displayed the inefficiency of the established music industry. So do the new fintech start-ups. They offer the same services as the incumbents but at a fraction of the price. They will win, but the fintech victory will not happen overnight. It will happen gradually as a new generation of consumers comes of age.

I believe that we have to operate with at least three scenarios when we plan our future.

The X scenario involves Generation X – people above the age of 35 with an established economy and established relations with their bank. They are modern people who will adjust to a more digital environment, as will their banks. But, seen as a whole, the scenario will shrink over time. Unless the incumbent banks do something– and I don't see them preparing anything – this will be an aging scenario.

The Y scenario is much more dynamic. Here we find the millennials – the biggest generation ever, with two billion people worldwide. The millennials are a hybrid generation. They operate partly in the X scenario and partly in their own Y scenario. Many have normal jobs but don't expect the same long corporate careers as their parents. They are financially less secure that their parents, they have a stressful 24-hour lifestyle and have to adjust to new technologies. They will increasingly live in the gig economy and rely on new fintech tools such as crowdfunding, crypto currencies and peer-to-peer lending. They turn their back on incumbent banks and seek new online banks instead. They do not pursue career and money at any price but seek influence and personal development. They choose Uber and Airbnb before taxis and hotels. They would rather rent than buy – because they don't know what their job situation will be just a few months ahead. They are more global than any generation before them but they distrust big international companies. The millennials are the generation looking for new localism, as their parents' scenario offers too few opportunities for them and the way life is today.

The Z scenario is an open scenario and dependent on whether the millennials succeed in creating a new local economy or the prevailing global digital economy continues. The general discussion in recent years has been about the differences between the millennials versus the two older generations – Generation X and the baby boomers. But the really interesting question may be the differences between Y and Z. Generation Z is about 8 to 18 years old and a generation that has grown up with smartphones and social media; they are the mutants, they are online 24-7, they have a concentration span of eight seconds – which is three seconds shorter than goldfish. Or maybe it's an eight-second information filter that enables them to evaluate its importance before they process the next message. They are a generation of people who have never been in a bank or read a newspaper and don't have the faintest idea about how to take out a loan.

Katniss Everdeen from the film *Hunger Games* is a typical Generation Z role model. She is alone in a fierce competition with only one winner, just like The X-Factor, Paradise Hotel and the business angels' accelerator programmes. Look at the series on Netflix, HBO and Amazon Prime: they are all about dystopias. While their grandparents grew out of the flower power of San Francisco, the Generation Zs of the Western world grow out of Silicon Valley's tech world, and they don't feel they really have a happy outlook if we continue the global digital economy.

What kind of society will we prepare for Generation Z when they have to manage on their own in five to ten years' time? We can let Silicon Valley set the agenda for another decade, or we can live up to our responsibility and create a strong new local economy. But that means that we have to dream better and bigger dreams!

15

WORK IS WHAT
DREAMS ARE
MADE ON

A 2013 study from Oxford University predicts that half of all jobs will disappear over the next 20 years. Even if we come to live in a jobless world, we may still be able to work with challenges and projects that give us personal satisfaction. At a conference on AI in Venice in 2018, Professor Mischa Dohler of King's College London claimed that AI would set us all free, as machines would do all the tedious work and allow human creativity to bloom.

I'm not that optimistic; some people may have a creative personality that makes it easy for them to find their own purpose in life, but that doesn't go for the majority. Most of us come from a culture where working is a virtue. I have a protestant background, where hard work is close to being the purpose of life and we cannot, over the coming 20 years, erase 2,000 years of working culture – and I suppose I get support from the majority of other cultures on the planet. In short, most of us want to work and when we don't do it, something goes wrong.

In the 1970s, Youngstown, Ohio closed down its steelworks and 50,000 lost their jobs. In the 1990s, it had built four new prisons. A jobless life caused a cultural, social and psychological meltdown for the people of Youngstown. It wasn't only about money; it was about losing a meaningful life, including one's pride in being able to provide for oneself. The Finnish government tried to introduce citizen wages, but given it up.

Therefore, we mustn't give in to a tech elite and solve unemployment with food coupons and Netflix. If people want a job, they shall have it. Over the next 12 years, we will add one billion more people on this planet, so creating a hi-tech society, which has an inherent purpose of making people dispensable, simply doesn't make sense. And for two reasons: first, it isn't what people want. Ask them and they will tell you they want good jobs. For the last century, women have fought for their right to have good well-paying jobs; we shouldn't create a society that produces no jobs and sends people home to update their Facebook. Second, if a company invests in new technology, which enables them to sack ten employees, that doesn't mean ten people cease to exist in the equation. They are still there, and if they can't find a new job, they become the responsibility of the rest of society.

I asked the mayor of a small municipality near Copenhagen what it was worth for the community to get unemployed people back into work, and his short answer was £13,000 a year. This is the price of disruption that venture capitalists ignore. That's the difference between a working and a non-working citizen – a happy and an unhappy human being, a productive and an unproductive worker.

I don't think we should condemn venture capitalists for disrupting industries or complain about companies that fire people to protect their business, but we have to stop expecting them to save the world and start getting ambitious instead.

In some cities, Airbnb has increased the total number of rooms being rented by 20%, which is generally seen as a challenge or a problem for the hotel industry. But it doesn't have to be. If people travel 20% more it's not a problem, and then Airbnb is an opportunity for more people to see the world. If technology eliminates 50% of all existing jobs, we need new dreams that are twice as big, and if a financial institution can do what it does today with just a quarter of its present staff, then it needs to grow its ambition four times. The future is not about sharing the values or the jobs we have already created, it's about creating a new world that doesn't look a bit like the old. We need an entirely new, sustainable global infrastructure for mobility, energy, manufacturing, food, health, culture and education. As Ezra Pound told Hemingway: "Make it new!"

And this new future growth starts locally. It starts with individuals who have ambitions. Cynthia Shanmugalingam could beat an established bank with more money because of her ambition and new financial technologies that enabled her to get funding from hundreds of small investors. Local Motors could challenge an incumbent motor industry that is a thousand times bigger thanks to new technologies that enable them to crowdsource talent and manufacture through 3D printing. Size doesn't matter anymore; it's just in the way, and economies of scale have unscaled.

The only things that really matter are dreams and actions. I once read an interview with the Swedish runner Susanna Kallur after she had set a world record: "I never imagined I would once become a world record holder when I started to run, I just wanted to run!" Dreams start small and develop over time and so do the big businesses of the future: they start as small dreams that grow out of small communities.

For as long as I can remember, the challenge for businesses has been to predict the future and adjust to it. That is not the case anymore. We cannot predict the future because the opportunities are too many, which is why so many have difficulties making strategic decisions – how can you develop a strategy when you don't know what to expect of the future? And this is where dreaming comes into the equation. If you have a dream, you know what you want with your future and then it's possible to devise a strategy.

16

A NEW KIND OF FINANCIAL ADVISOR FOR THE NEW LOCAL ECONOMY

I was at a presentation, "Unlocking the Secrets to Raising Millions on Kickstarter and Indiegogo," at the Google for Startups Campus in London, which is in the heart of Tech City and a place where you find new interesting trends. The speaker was Khierstyn Ross from Toronto, a crowdfunding advisor who over the last couple of years has advised young entrepreneurs on how to dig up funding for their start-ups. The next generation of self-employed people have long given up on going to the banks – a loan from the bank is not even on their radar. They can't get it, and they don't want to.

Traditionally, if you had the idea of manufacturing your own design for a smart fingerprint padlock, for instance, you would go to the bank and get a loan that made it possible to manufacture the product before you started to market and sell it. With crowdfunding, this process is reversed. But your backers are more than just investors. Very often they help you market your product as well, because they feel ownership of the product.

I once backed a crowdfunding project for a fancy red smartwatch, and I have talked about 'my' watch at numerous speeches and know of at least five people who have bought it.

This is what Elon Musk did when he presented his Tesla 3 on 1 April 2016: two days after the presentation, he had more than a quarter of a million pre-orders worth more than $10 billion – and all he had was a prototype! It's mega-crowdfunding.

With crowdfunding marketing, funding and sales are integrated in the same process before manufacturing. The risk profile is completely different from normal financing. As a crowdfunding advisor, Ross helps her clients get funding – exactly as the bank used to – but unlike traditional financial advisors, she also assists with marketing and sales as an integrated part of her service.

A lot of people – myself included – think that crowdfunding is only about getting a good idea and uploading a short video on the crowdfunding site. Wrong! The world is full of bright ideas and no one is just discovered. It takes a lot of intelligent work. Before you go online, you need to have the first backers ready, explains Ross. You also need to have a crowd of your own ready on social media before you start your campaign. That was not the case for the clothing company Thin Ice when it wanted to launch its clothes that would help you to lose weight. As a result, the company only got $16,000, which was far too little.

Then Ross stepped in. She created a new avatar for the key customer, built a big audience on social media and timed the campaign so that Thin Ice was included in Kickstarter and Indiegogo's newsletters, and the campaign was wildly overfunded with $600,000.

If you have a clever crowdfunding advisor like Ross, why would you need a bank? Or let me reframe the question: If you have a clever bank advisor who knows what crowdfunding is all about and can advise you on marketing on social media – why would you need Ross?

New financial technologies are about to shape the coming generation of local entrepreneurs for whom a tool like crowdfunding is the new normal and not the exception. This is why we are beginning to see the first crowdfunding advisors claiming the grey area between funding and branding. Only a few professionals are occupying the new field at the moment, but there will be more, including a lot of reinvented advisors and consultants we haven't even thought of yet.

I believe this is a new opportunity for community banks and local bank branches. What Ross does, banks should be able to do too, and I asked a banker why crowdfunding advice wasn't already part of their local service portfolio. If you dare not give them a loan, why don't you help them get funded by the crowd? I got the answer: "We bankers are not marketing and branding experts!" Well, neither was Ross a few years ago; she left university with a bachelors' degree in biochemistry, but since then has helped start-ups get $4 million worth of funding.

I believe that community banks and financial institutions with local branches need to reinvent themselves. Being local does not in and of itself secure your future. Clever reinterpretation does. Shakespeare wrote *Hamlet* more than four centuries ago, and yet it is still the most performed play in the world today. How can that be? My guess is because the play is constantly reinterpreted. Theatre companies don't play *Hamlet* as they did in the Globe in 1603; they transfer the play into new and modern settings. The main story is the same, but it is told in a way that brings it in sync with today. No one would be surprised if some director decided to use the White House as a setting for a modern *Hamlet* with Hillary Clinton as Gertrude – or would she be the murdered king?

I have facilitated a number of 'local banking hacks' in London. They are a kind of hackathon where bankers are asked to radically reinvent local banking over two days. One team suggested that community banks stop their focus on what they could do for their customers and instead concentrate on what their customers could do for each other. As one team said: "If a bank has to reject a loan to a business customer because the project seems too risky, it doesn't mean that the bank cannot help the customer. We can't give you a loan, but we can connect you with potential customers that may be interested in collaborating with you." Banks have so much information about their customers and, as it is today, they only think of it as a marketing and sales tool. If they pursued a role as network facilitator, they could become the future operating system for local economy and global communities. Banks could be the future platforms for new business communities and provide access to fresh resources – not just money but talent, suppliers and customers. Almost all successful businesses in the 21st century are based on platforms – why not the next generation of reinterpreted banks too?

One of the teams in the banking hackathon suggested that banks should even offer an online dating service: *We help you find a boyfriend with money!* I agree that it sounds far-fetched, and bankers were quick to reject the idea, but maybe there is some sense in this line of thinking. People may not like banks, but they trust their information and a huge problem on dating sites is lack of trust.

One in three millennials use dating sites. You may compare new banking products to add-on items in petrol stations. Half a century ago, petrol stations made their money selling petrol and oil; now 70% of their profit comes from food, drinks, sweets and "pink sunglasses", as the owner of one station said.

I won't defend online dating as a banking service to my death, but I will emphasize the opportunities that lie in community banks providing a framework for local business. Last year British banks closed down almost 1,000 branches, while new co-working spaces popped up across the UK, catering for 1.7 million freelancers. We may not need a branch for banking anymore, but we need a space and a community for our small businesses.

NEW LOCAL ECONOMY MUST COMPETE WITH SILICON VALLEY

In 1881, a 23-year-old dairyman, Jacob Stilling-Andersen, participated in a winter course for modern dairy production at Tune Agricultural School in Denmark. The young man was impressed with what he learned and when he returned to his village, he suggested that the local farmers found their own dairy plant. At that time, there were two kinds of butter in Denmark, the butter produced by the small farmers themselves and that produced at dairy plants at the manors. The latter was of a far better quality and was sold at a price 50% higher.

Stilling-Andersen suggested to the local farmers that they collect their milk but not produce the butter individually. Instead they should treat the milk in a new plant that was to be mutually owned by the farmers. What had inspired the young man to suggest this was a new and advanced centrifuge he had learned about on his dairy course. The new piece of machinery was called the Maglekilde Centrifuge, which separates milk into cream and skimmed milk much more cheaply and efficiently and, as a result, produces better-quality butter at a lower cost.

None of the small farmers could afford to buy the centrifuge by themselves, but if they bought it together, they would be able to compete with the manors. In 1882 his plan was realized and Denmark got its first dairy cooperative, Hjedding Andelsmejeri. Ten years later, in 1892, the country had 679 dairy cooperatives and by 1904 the number had grown to 1,168. During this time, the number of manor dairies dropped from 283 to 89.

In just one decade, during the 19th century, Denmark's 100,000 small poor farmers had completely outperformed 2,000 rich manor owners on the butter market thanks to a new technology and by adopting a cooperative mindset. The importance of the Maglekilde Centrifuge cannot be underestimated; it made Denmark the dairy country it is today. Most of the cooperatives have merged and consolidated over the last century into what today is Arla Foods, the sixth largest dairy producer in the world. Even today, it is still owned by 12,000 farmers. Had all this been achieved today, more than a century later, we would probably have said that the Scandinavian states had been created through crowdfunding.

The ideas from the dairy industry spread across the entire country. The biggest Danish supermarket chain is today a cooperative owned by consumers; many banks and building societies are owned by the customers and so are several insurance companies. The cooperative mindset that grew out of small agricultural communities has to a very large extent permeated Danish society and become the inspiration for the modern Scandinavian welfare model, where members of a community get rich together and not at the expense of someone else. The lesson from the Danish cooperatives involve at least four elements:

- **New technology**: It was the Maglekilde Centrifuge and other inventions of times that made change possible.
- **Collaboration**: The small farmers could not afford to buy the new technology by themselves. They all

had to chip in, and they were willing to do so for the common good.

- **Social equality**: All members of the cooperative had one vote regardless of their share in the new production facility.

- **Education**: The cooperative mindset was founded on education: all people should be well informed in order to make sound decisions for the community. The first dairy cooperative was a direct result of a young man learning about new technology and modern farming.

The story of the Danish dairy cooperatives is extremely encouraging, I think. It shows that if we create strong local economies and cooperate, we can create businesses that are as competitive – if not more competitive – than both bigger and wealthier companies.

The future starts small and local.

TEN BASIC RULES IN THE NEW LOCAL AND COMMUNITY ECONOMY

1. **Start with a fresh dream**: This is where your future energy and passion will come from. Your dream doesn't have to be big, it will grow as you go along; but it has to be original and it has to be yours. If it isn't your dream, make it yours.
2. **Make it new**: Don't try to fix what you already have. Discard old thinking and old technology and start with a clean slate. Times are changing, and you have to design new solutions from scratch to get the trends on your side.
3. **Redefine the community identity**: You need to understand and be integrated in your community and be part of its culture. Analyse the three Rs – rituals, relations and restrictions – that identify your new business opportunities.
4. **Involve your crowd**: Your community is not your customers; they are your partners who will help you get funding, they will provide the talent your need, they will help you market the business and eventually buy your products.
5. **Small is beautiful**: Create a distributed economy based on lots of small units and design an organization that will enable all the units to work together. And then start to collaborate with other businesses just like yours.

6. **Be interested in new technology**: Make a decision to be excited about new solutions. Technology is developing exponentially and practically all progress is created by new technology. Old age isn't an excuse for not being interested.
7. **Make an *unscaled* new business**: Economy of scale is no longer an advantage. New technology enables small local companies to develop and manufacture premium goods faster and better than global companies.
8. **Mind the gap**: If you are already an established company on the market, you need to reinterpret your history and redefine your business in order to cross the technology gap. Stick to your history but tell it in a new and modern way.
9. **Trust human intelligence**: The tech world is full of AI and big data, but new ideas and progress are created by human intelligence. Spend more time with your community than your computer.
10. **Go on an expedition**: Don't waste time predicting the future but trust your dream. The future may seem chaotic, but that is only because you haven't met it yet. As a small and nimble company, you will solve problems as you meet them.